How to Adult, A Practical Guide

How to Adult,

A Practical Guide

Advice on Living, Loving,
Working, and Spending
Like a Grown-Up

JAMIE GOLDSTEIN, PSYD

ROCKRIDGE
PRESS

For general information on our other products and services or to obtain technical support, please contact our Customer Care Department within the United States at (866) 744-2665, or outside the United States at (510) 253-0500.

Rockridge Press publishes its books in a variety of electronic and print formats. Some content that appears in print may not be available in electronic books, and vice versa.

TRADEMARKS: Rockridge Press and the Rockridge Press logo are trademarks or registered trademarks of Callisto Media Inc. and/or its affiliates, in the United States and other countries, and may not be used without written permission. All other trademarks are the property of their respective owners. Rockridge Press is not associated with any product or vendor mentioned in this book.

Interior and Cover Designer: Brieanna Felschow
Art Producer: Samantha Ulban
Editors: Marisa A. Hines and Nora Spiegel
Production Editor: Rachel Taenzler
Author photo courtesy of Sarah Matista Photography.
ISBN: Print 978-1-64739-721-0 | eBook 978-1-64739-425-7
R0

To my Sissy.

As you adult like you mean it,
I see you.

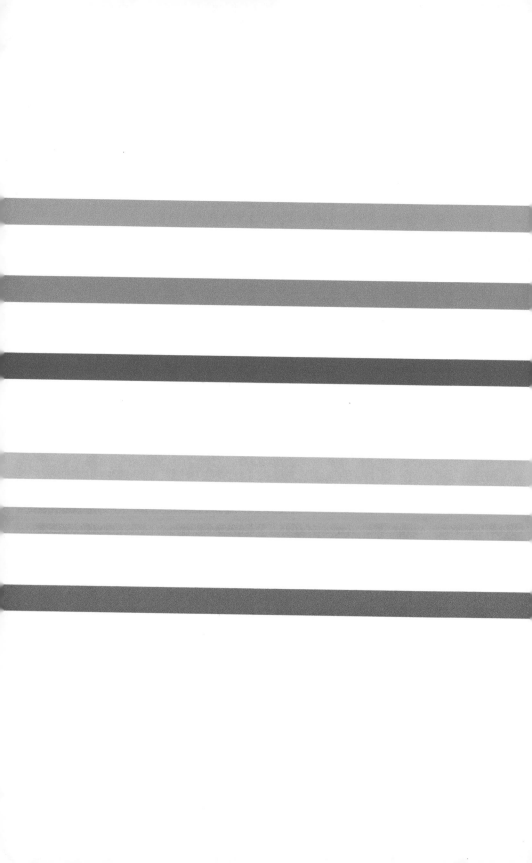

Contents

INTRODUCTION   IX

CHAPTER ONE: So, You Opened up   1
This Book...

CHAPTER TWO: Get Started by Forgetting   23
about Everyone Else

CHAPTER THREE: Relationships (Because You   47
Can Only Forget about
Everyone Else for So Long)

CHAPTER FOUR: How to Kill It at Work   77

CHAPTER FIVE: I Just Found Five Dollars   101
in My Pocket!

CHAPTER SIX: How to Adult Like You   123
Mean It

RESOURCES   139

VALUES   143

REFERENCES   145

INDEX   147

Introduction

So, here you are. You made it through your teens, you've success-
fully been able to walk into a bar with your head held high because
you're using your own ID, and you possibly are trying—or thinking
about trying—to live life out in the "real world." Let's be real about
this "real world" situation for a second; as exciting and awesome as it
is that the world is now your oyster, that's one big oyster. And while
oysters do make pearls, they can also be nearly impossible to crack
open, not to mention that they come with a whole lot of slimy stuff.
That's where this gem of a book comes in. Consider it the knife with
which you shuck that oyster wide open, and the knowledge you gain
is the lemon or hot sauce to help that oyster go down smoothly.

But enough seafood talk. The truth is, getting further into your 20s
means getting further into the world of adulting. It's tough out there,
and the struggle is real. What's more is you're moving swiftly into
adulting during a day and age that looks light-years different from
the adulting of past generations. A major factor in the creation of this
book was to speak to the nuanced and complex parts of adulting that
haven't been addressed before. Though the basics of domestic life,
hygiene, and how to find work are important, this book is intended
to support you beyond the basics. What you'll find in these pages are

insights written to reflect today's modern challenges, from relationship transitions to finding the right budgeting app.

This book is meant to act as a map, with me as your guide at the helm. Why me? Well, a couple of reasons: First, I am someone who is very actively adulting, and who I promise is not as old as whoever raised you, and second, I'm a psychologist (aka therapist) who, day in and day out, works with folks who are finding their own paths to adulting. With that sort of personal and professional experience, one could argue that I definitely know my stuff. Part of that stuff is knowing that, as cool as it may seem to be aloof or a lone wolf who is always unfazed, life doesn't actually work that way. Humans are social creatures who need to be connected to others. None of us are meant to go it alone, especially when learning, exploring, and transitioning into new parts of our lives. The hope, dear reader, is to leave you feeling empowered with a few nuggets of real-life tips, tricks, and tools you need to stay true to you while adulting like you mean it.

"It is surprising to notice that even from the earliest age, man finds the greatest satisfaction in feeling independent. The exalting feeling of being sufficient to oneself comes as a revelation."

—Maria Montessori

CHAPTER ONE

So, You Opened up This Book...

Whether you're pumped about adulting or not, the transition into adulthood is unavoidable. But it isn't all bad. To start, let's keep things simple and sweet by honoring how you arrived at a book like this one. Along the way, we will cover one of the quintessential struggles of adulting, which is that everyone has an opinion about it. It's easy to end up caught between taking in those opinions and attempting to establish one of your own. Fear not, though—this book contains a fun little quiz that will help you identify what it is that *you* want from this whole adulting thing. I invite you to start thinking about what flavors of change you want to see, hear, and feel within yourself. While I am here to guide you, it will be *your* truth that we will use as a compass.

If This Book Was Given to You by an Overbearing Family Member or Friend . . .

Oh…hi there. So sorry we're meeting like this. I know this may not have been your first choice for Sunday afternoon entertainment or the way you wanted to relax before bed, but since we both happen to be here…maybe we should give this thing a go?

As great as loved ones are, sometimes the ways they give or show their love aren't quite how we want to receive it. Regardless of their intention, the gesture of someone handing you a book on adulting may leave you feeling slighted. It could feel like their way of telling you that you're doing a crappy job and really need to step up your game. It could feel like they're attempting to impose their thoughts and opinions on what you should be doing and how you should be doing it. It could even feel like their way of subtly telling you that they disapprove of your current way of being in the world and want you to make life changes that they'll approve of. Whatever the impact, I want you to know that I see you. The goal in this book is to help you recognize the plethora of opinions offered to new adults like yourself for what they are—other people's opinions—and to take up space in your life by starting to form your own.

All that said, if we are going to throw shade at the presumptuous people in your life, it's also worthwhile to take into account their possible intentions. If this book was gifted to you by someone who is attempting to show you some love, what is it that they might be trying to say? Sure, their intention could be a subtle hint that they think you're totally blowing it...or maybe, just maybe, it's their way of saying, *"Hey, I see you over there. I get that figuring out who you are and how to do life is hard.* Maybe *this will help lighten the load."* As frustrating and confusing as it may be to constantly be on the receiving end of other people's opinions, remember that offering a perspective is also one way people try to look out for each other. Or maybe they really are just being a passive-aggressive a-hole! Either way, now you've got this tool in your hands that was made to help you solve situations like this one—dealing with the passive and not-so-passive opinion givers in your life.

There are *many* points of view out there, and taking all of them in can be confusing, frustrating, overwhelming...you name it. There is intention versus impact. There is also the question of whether, at the end of the day, all of the opinions thrown your way are truly worth your time. Well...it depends. I know, I know, it might be a frustrating answer, but it's an honest one. Determining what to do with someone else's opinion is a challenging process because our relationships with other humans are complex. The relationship we have to someone impacts whether their opinion is weighted more heavily than others. If your high school English teacher was more mentor than teacher and you respected the way they ran their class, their opinion on how to move through adulthood might be one you take to heart. On the other end of the spectrum, if your auntie is someone who regularly has strong opinions that have never really jibed with yours, then her thoughts on how you're living your life might not hold nearly as much weight. If it all sounds complicated, that's because it can be. The good news is that it doesn't have to be. That's why this book has loads more on navigating all types of relationships coming your way in chapter 3. So, hold onto your hat—we are gearing up to dive right in. That said, if you simply cannot wait one more second…jump on ahead to chapter 3. It's your journey, after all, and this book doesn't have to be moved through in a linear fashion. Start with anything that's calling your name.

If *You* Were the One to Pick up This Book . . .

Oh, hell yeah! If I could high-five or fist-bump you, I would. Picking up a book like this is a major step to take for yourself, and it is always impressive when anyone out there looks for ways to get their personal growth on. Showing up for yourself is a major part of this whole adulting thing, and you're already doing it. This likely means you're looking for answers to some big questions, such as:

- How do I *actually* take care of myself?

- What do I do when family, friends, and partners are pissing me off?

- What do I do when I finally get a job but realize it's sucking the life out of me?

- I know I need to make money and save money, but what about all the details?

Questions like these don't simply pop up on everybody's 21st birthday. For some, they are a slow build, whereas for others they are a bit more of a smack in the face. However the questions arise, they tend to stem from two sources: the inside and the outside. The outside pressures can look like those overbearing loved ones who might have given you this book in the first place, but they can also look like YouTube, Instagram stories, Netflix, Hulu, Snapchat, billboard ads, or any other big source of messaging. Another way of saying it is that there are a lot of outside sources, on both the interpersonal and institutional scale, that could be inviting you to feel the pressure to "adult" better.

Then, of course, there are the inside sources that bring on pressures to get answers to the big questions. These are the voices in your head and heart. Sometimes the voice can be a harsh ribbing telling you, *"Figure it out already!"* and other times the voice can be the encouraging excitement telling you, *"Get out there and be the awesome adult person you know you're capable of being."*

When your internal voice is coming at you sideways, it's helpful to understand the potential fears that could be driving it. In my work with individuals who are learning their way through the world of adulting, I regularly hear, *"But what if I'm doing it wrong?!"* If a fear of adulting wrong is what sparked your interest in this book, I have great news for you:

1. This book will help guide you in a direction that feels solid.

2. The fact that you even picked up this book is proof that you're already on the right track.

Regardless of how this book found its way into your hands, getting the most out of it requires a willingness to learn. In the world of psychology, there is a theory about the impact of someone's mindset when it comes to their ability to grow. The badass psychologist Carol Dweck did a bunch of research that shows how powerful a "growth mindset" can be in comparison to what she calls a "fixed mindset." A fixed mindset is exactly what it sounds like: seeing your abilities as set in their ways. When we say things like, *"Oh, I'm not a math person,"* that's a fixed mindset. On the other side of the coin is a growth mindset: seeing yourself and your abilities as capable of growth and change.

When it comes to adulting, taking on a growth mindset can be super helpful because at the end of the day, you *are* growing, learning, and transforming. It doesn't matter who you are, where you come from, or what is going on in your personal life…everyone is capable of viewing their experiences through a lens of growth and change. As you start moving through the chapters of this book, remember to step into your own growth mindset.

LET'S START WITH A QUIZ

When we embark on any journey of self-growth and evolution, we have to first know where we're starting. Without knowing where you're at, how would you know that you were going anywhere, let alone in the direction you want to be going? This quiz will help you identify that starting point by taking a look at some of the big-ticket adulting items. A typical BuzzFeed quiz might ask if you know how to change a tire or iron a shirt. However, we know there's more to adulting than that. That's why we are looking at adult things like your general sense of health (physical, mental, *and* emotional), how comfortable you feel navigating money basics, the various relationships you have (family, friends, romantic, etc.), what sort of thoughts you have about work/career, and, of course, how rooted you feel in knowing who you are as a whole person.

JUST HOW "ADULT" AM I? QUIZ

1. Do I know how to tune into my body?

    a. Yes! I am one with my body.

    b. Maybe? I know that spicy food gives me a stomachache.

    c. I can't think about my body right now, I'm just trying to get it out of bed . . .

2. Do I treat my body kindly?

    a. My body is a temple—only the purest things enter it.

    b. Sometimes my body wants to go hard; sometimes it wants to veg out.

    c. Taco Bell at 2:00 a.m. is my nightly jam! I'll sleep when I'm dead.

3. How do I think about myself?

    a. I am a gift to all of humanity!

    b. Blech, I am not a fan of me.

    c. Meh, I'm alright, I guess . . .

4. How do I think about others/the world?

    a. The world is terrifying, and people suck!

    b. The world is an awesome place, and people are the best!

    c. There's a world out there?

5. Do I know how to calm my mind when it's spinning out?

    a. I can hardly sit when I'm spinning out—there's no way I can be calm.

    b. I'm a Zen master!

    c. If there's a dog around and I can rub its belly, I'm chill.

6. Do I know how to express my feels?

    a. Express them?! Hell no, too scary. I barely know what feelings are.

    b. In a text, maybe.

    c. If I'm feeling a certain way, everyone and their mother know it.

7. What's my basic understanding of credit cards?

    a. Cha-ching! I can buy things now and worry about paying later (or never).

    b. What the heck is a credit score even for?

    c. I have a credit card, but I'm too scared to use it.

8. Do I feel like I know what I need in order to start saving money?

    a. Totally! 401(k)s, IRAs, rainy-day funds . . . I am prepared!

    b. Umm . . . yeah . . . no.

    c. I've got a savings account. Isn't that enough?

9. How would I describe my family boundaries?

    a. Boundaries *shmoundaries*. I tell them everything.

    b. I am a brick wall. They can't know anything about me

    c. I share plenty with them, and there's some stuff they don't need to know.

10. Do my friends bring me life?

    a. I don't think I could survive without them!

    b. They're okay to hang out with, but I don't always like it.

    c. I don't have enough of them to know.

11. Would I date me?

    a. I wish I could! I am a gift to humanity, remember?

    b. Nah, I'm too much this and too little that.

    c. I'm not perfect, but I think I make a good partner.

12. When I imagine working, do I get pumped for a particular thing?

    a. I know exactly what direction I'm going in.

    b. I have no idea where I'm going.

    c. I'm still learning what I get pumped about.

13. If asked, do I know where I shine and where I can use more polish?

    a. I'm all shine, baby! No dullness here.

    b. Shine? I don't think so.

    c. I definitely know what I'm good at *and* where I have room to grow.

14. Can I name my biggest fears?

    a. Sure, I can get real about my fears.

    b. Hell no, that's why they are fears! Too scary to talk about.

    c. Maybe—depends on how deep we are about to get.

15. Can I name my biggest points of pride in myself?

    a. Definitely, I have a few things to be really proud of.

    b. I don't think I've done much to be proud of (yet).

    c. No way, that would make me sound so full of myself.

QUIZ RESULTS AND EXPLANATION

If many of your answers lean toward a general sense of *"I have no idea,"* keep reading. On the other hand, if a lot of them lean toward *"I know everything and got this on lock,"* still keep reading! Either starting point is worth getting curious about.

If after taking this quiz you notice you responded mostly with answers that make you feel like you're slaying the adulting game already, that's awesome. This suggests that you are well on your way. However, it does not suggest that your journey is over or that you've learned all there is and should stop now. I want you feeling confident in who you are and where you're at, but I certainly would not want you to miss out on the potential to go deeper in your process. Take the time to read back over some of the questions and ask yourself where you might have room to grow and expand. When it comes down to it, there's no such thing as being "done." In fact, my hope for you is that you never arrive. If you feel like you've "made it," check again. To be alive is to be ever -evolving. If you are feeling dope about where you're at, that's great, but don't forget to ask yourself where you want to go next.

On the other hand, if after taking the quiz you've ended up with more of an "oh crap" mentality, hear me when I say that there is no reason to start tripping. What this suggests is your path might actually be more clear-cut. Most folks who are starting out on their adulting journey walk into it with boatloads of questions and uncertainties. It isn't your job to have all the answers—now or ever. Read back through the quiz and see what questions stand out most to you. Which ones strike you as a little more exciting? Which ones seem a little scarier? These answers will help you start to see the way forward.

Whatever your answers are, trust that they are guiding you to a starting point that is just right for you. One of the all-too-common assumptions about adulting is that everybody should be at a similar place by a similar time. While there are some basic essentials that everyone can stand to learn more about, *there is no one-size-fits-all model*. Humans vary widely, and it is good that they do. Imagine how boring it would be if everyone had the same struggles and the same victories in the same way at the same time. Blech!

How to Handle Others When Figuring Out Your Own Life

In the early stages of figuring out your own life, you will undoubtedly encounter other people's thoughts on the matter. Everyone's got an opinion about everything, and learning to navigate among all these opinions is a key component to holding your own as an adult. Handling others isn't so tough when they agree with you, support you, and are 100 percent in accordance. But when the agreement, support, and accord start lacking is when the real work begins. Some questions you can start to ask yourself when navigating other people's opinions are:

- **Whose opinions do you trust?**

  ↳ Identify the handful of people you admire and trust. Make these the folks you go to when feeling confused or unsure.

- **What are the expectations you might have of other people's opinions?**

  ↳ If you expect people will always agree with what you are doing, you are bound to be disappointed.

- **What is this person telling you about themselves or their views?**

  ↳ When someone offers an opinion, they are sharing with you their view on themselves and the world around them. Sometimes someone's opinion says more about them than it does about you.

- **How do you feel about disagreement?**

  ↳ Remember that you don't always have to see eye to eye with someone. In fact, having a difference in opinions can both strengthen your relationship with that person and expand your worldview.

As you begin to step more fully into your own opinions, the ability to set boundaries becomes one of the best tools for keeping you safe and sane when you bump up against differing opinions, feelings, and desires. Don't be afraid to start asserting some of your own boundaries when things get heated. One of the simplest ways is to segue to a new topic. In other words, feel free to redirect the conversation to move away from something that feels too hot.

WHERE DO YOU WANT TO MAKE CHANGES?

While very few things in life are guaranteed, what is known beyond a shadow of a doubt is that change is inevitable. Whether you are making a conscious effort to play a part in it or hanging back while it all goes down, the change will come. If it is going to happen anyway with the passage of time, why not be an active participant in your own change?

Looking through the earlier quiz results, what change do you start to envision for yourself? If you were to show the quiz and results to your auntie, brother, or boss, they would likely have all sorts of ideas on what changes you could and should be making. But, as will be said over and over in this book (in fact, that's what the next chapter is about), this adulting thing is not about your mother, brother, boss, besties, bros, or bartender. It is about *you*. So, with that in mind, get those gears turning and think about the changes that matter most to you.

I invite you to start by making a list of these changes. You can begin by reflecting on your answers to the quiz, but don't feel like you have to limit yourself. Reach beyond those quiz categories. You are the expert on you, which means you are the only one who can decide what your wants, needs, desires, and dreams are. Well, except for the basics like food, water, rest, shelter, and love. Trust me, you need these. We *all* need these. As you start to conjure up your list of changes, try not to dive too deep into the "Holy sh*t, I need to change *everything*" rabbit hole. The list is not meant to overwhelm you but rather to excite you and be the guiding compass to orient you when you're not quite sure where else to go.

CHANGES I WANT TO MAKE

_____

_____

_____

_____

_____

_____

_____

_____

_____

_____

_____

_____

_____

_____

While moving through the different parts of this book, you can come back to your list and take stock of what changes might fit where. For example, if you want to change your spending habits, hold on to that desire for change while reading through chapter 5. Maybe you're having a tough time with certain family members (or all of them); note the changes you want to make happen with them, and see if you can bring some of those changes to life while you make your way through chapter 3.

This book is loaded with legit tips and tricks for you to pull from when taking real steps toward making some real change. That said, it might not have every answer to every question you have. Don't forget to be your own explorer. If any of the changes you want to make are specific or personal to you (e.g., "*I want to come out to the world about an aspect of my identity*"), first and foremost, hell yeah! Second, start to think about how you want to bring this change to life in a way that's realistic and doable for you. Your list is about mapping out where you want to go. From there, you can find the pathways toward the change and enjoy the heck out of that journey. If you find that things begin to shift along the way, that's completely okay. It is all part of the adulting process.

A Moment of Reflection

Let's recap! You are here because you or someone who knows you wants to support you in adulting like you mean it.

+ This book is not a doom-and-gloom guide to adulthood; it's here to support your adulting journey in a way that feels right for *you*… with a giggle or two thrown in, of course.

+ You now have a gauge of where you're at in your adulting process across a handful of different categories, such as physical and mental health, money, and relationships.

+ You came up with a list of changes to guide you toward living *your* best life.

"Change will not come if we wait for some other person or if we wait for some other time. We are the ones we've been waiting for. We are the change that we seek."

—Barack Obama

CHAPTER TWO

Get Started by Forgetting about Everyone Else

Remember how I mentioned that everyone's got an opinion and that part of adulting is navigating people and their two cents? Well, for this moment, you can forget all that noise. I'm not saying you have to completely disown and remove folks from your life, but it is important to start with the things you can do to truly care for *you*. That is why in this chapter we are 100 percent focused on you: your mind, your physical body, and refining that list you made through this all-about-you lens. First, let's start with understanding what it *really* means to do you.

Focus on You

When people talk about focusing on themselves, a word you often hear is *selfish*. Statements like *"I feel like I'm being selfish"* or *"I don't want to be selfish"* get used a lot. While those sentiments are legit because acting selfishly can be quite the bummer, it's worth looking at the idea of "selfishness" a little bit closer to notice what else might be there.

We're often told that focusing on oneself in any way, shape, or form is a bad thing. Not true! In this book, I challenge this notion by highlighting the important difference between selfishness and self-focus. For the record, I'm not saying being selfish is the ideal way to be. By definition, *selfish* describes a person who is not considerate of others and is focused only on their own profit or pleasure. Self-focus, on the other hand, does not imply negligence or harm the same way selfishness does. Self-focus means honoring the reality that you, too, have needs and that meeting them is a necessary part of your well-being. Unfortunately, these two very different approaches often get lumped together, inviting us to feel guilty when we do what we have to do to meet our own needs. The good news is that as you learn to adult, you can learn to un-lump these ideas.

Focusing on yourself does not have to mean copping an attitude or putting on blinders to everyone around you. Prioritizing you simply means honoring your own needs and allowing them to take up space. A few things have to happen for this to occur:

1. Eliminating clutter in the form of other people's wants/needs/opinions.

2. Tuning in to yourself to identify what your needs actually are.

3. Finding healthy ways to get those needs met as best as you can.

To clear clutter, we usually need some tools and a game plan. Imagine you were to clean out a section of a living space, like a closet or a garage. You'd get tools such as garbage bags, boxes, and maybe some Lysol to clean up the dust. You'd also devise some sort of game plan, like what things to toss, donate, or keep and rearrange. Clearing the clutter that other people put on us is no different: In order to focus on ourselves, we need the right tools and a solid game plan.

Start with thinking about the various things that seem to be crowding your ability to do you. This might be a parent telling you to get off the couch and get a job. This might be an uncle pushing you to finish that mechanics program so you can come work in his shop. It could be friends telling you to join them on the law school train. It could even be someone encouraging you to follow a dream they *think* you have. Whatever tone the clutter takes, allow yourself to recognize it. Go through some of the messages you're receiving and see what you'd like to hold on to for later use and what you'd like to go ahead and toss out. If it's not resonating with you or bringing you joy, toss it right out. By doing so, you can make more space for what *you* want from your adult self.

With the clutter from others removed, you now have lots more space for your wants, needs, hopes, dreams, dance moves, inventions—whatever you want to fill that space with! There are many ways to start formulating and tuning in to your own wants and needs. One of my favorite ways is by identifying your values. Values are those little bits of magic we can stand by and say, "*This* matters to me." Regardless of what is happening around you, your values are a personal anchor that can offer true guidance and clarity on your everyday wants and needs. Examples of values include open-mindedness, freedom, and humor. Take a look at the back of this book for a go-to list of values (page 143) that you can use to start identifying what it is that you truly need for yourself as opposed to what the clutter was trying to convince you that you need.

Once you've identified a value and a need that feels true to you, it's time to start to get those needs met for real. Two ways to empower yourself to meet your own needs are to focus on your mind and focus on your body. Let's say that a value of yours is courage and that the need you have is to engage with that sense of courageousness. You're going to find it awfully hard to get that need met if you're not actively caring of your mind and body. When your mental and/or physical health feels out of sorts, it's really hard to feel any sense of awesome. I got you, though! Keep reading to see how you can start focusing on *you* and stop focusing on all that clutter.

Take Care of Your Mind

As the great Mahatma Gandhi said, *"You can chain me, you can torture me, you can even destroy this body, but you will never imprison my mind."* Hopefully, you're not at the point of experiencing torture, but there is something powerful in his statement of what it means to care for your mind. Your mind is something that is solely yours. It belongs to nobody else. For this reason, it's imperative to take extra good care of it.

The Importance of Staying Mentally Healthy

Real talk: Your mental health cannot be ignored. According to the results of countless research studies out of major organizations such as the Centers for Disease Control and Prevention and the National Institute of Mental Health, the important role mental health plays in well-being cannot be overstated. If you were to take a road trip, you'd regularly have to stop to fill the gas tank, right? Otherwise, you wouldn't be able to go anywhere. Or worse, you could end up stranded somewhere you definitely didn't want to spend that much time.

Staying mentally healthy is a lot like filling a car with gas: necessary to get where you're going and a natural part of the process. If you were in the car with a friend and they said, *"I have to stop for gas,"* you wouldn't judge them for being weird or think there was something "wrong" with them. You'd simply hang out in the passenger seat while they did what they needed to do. You might even offer to pitch in a little to help them fill up because, hey, you can't get to where you're going if their gas tank is empty the same way they couldn't get anywhere with you if you were on empty. When you let your mental and emotional well-being slide, it's like running on empty; you can't get very far.

If you notice yourself feeling particularly cranky, tired, nervous, or sad, there are three major ways to refuel your mental health: connection, rest, and asking for help. I know, I know, this whole chapter is about focusing on *you*. However, that doesn't mean completely isolating. In fact, staying mentally healthy requires the exact opposite. Humans are social animals; we are meant to be connected to other humans. So, when your tank is low, look around and see who you could be connecting with in ways that fill you up. Then there's resting up, which is more than simply sleep. It's taking the time to slow down, as opposed to that go-go-go lifestyle. Rest is about reminding yourself that not everything has to be a constant grind. Lastly, and this one is major: *Ask. For. Help.* This practice is vital to prioritizing yourself in a way that supports your mental health. Whether that means finding a local therapist in your area; checking in with your priest, rabbi, imam, or meditation teacher; setting up a one-on-one with your boss; or going to your favorite aunt, asking for help is one of the greatest fueling stations for mental and emotional health.

Meditation and Other Techniques

When it comes to matters of the mind, meditation is one fantastic practice. When the stress, anxiety, and general upset become too much, a meditation practice is one way to guide yourself back to the present. Another word that gets tossed around when people talk about meditation is *mindfulness*. Sometimes you even hear a combo where people talk about "mindfulness meditation." Really, it is about bringing yourself into the present moment and being aware of the fact that you're in it. In your very full day-to-day life, there is all kinds of stuff to think about: *"Did I lock the door when I left? How did that meeting go? Am I ever going to find someone to date? How long should I leave that in the oven? Does my haircut look weird?"* Question after question, thought after thought flow in and out of your mind, taking you away from the present moment you are in and keeping you from noticing things like your surroundings, your breath, and your physical body.

You might be picturing a bunch of people sitting crossed-legged in a room with their eyes closed in perfect silence and stillness, but this is just one of many ways to engage in a meditation practice. Other options include walking, writing, dancing, and eating. Meditation has been practiced for thousands of years in various Eastern cultures and more recently has gained popularity in the West. It has received so much recognition that it has even been adapted into technology as a helpful way to cultivate a daily practice. There are tons of fantastic apps (e.g., Calm, Headspace, and Insight Timer) available for your cell phone that can help guide you back into the present moment.

Engaging in a meditation practice is not the only way to tap into the present moment awareness and take care of your mental health. Activities like listening to music, viewing art, singing, journaling, reading, and exercise are all practices that encourage in-the-moment awareness. At the end of the day, the techniques to care for your mind are not about forcing your mind to go blank. In fact, that's pretty much impossible. Instead, think about giving yourself the chance to be with what *is* happening as opposed to getting caught up in what you think *could* or *should* be happening.

Moments of Introspection

In order to care for your mind, another practice becomes pretty damn important: the practice of introspection. Introspection is what allows you to get curious about how you operate on a mental and emotional level, and then use the knowledge to guide your daily life. Self-awareness increases anytime you take a moment to get curious about why you think what you think, feel what you feel, and act how you act. This whole process takes a lot of openness and even some hefty doses of objectivity, and let me tell you, sometimes it isn't easy to do. It takes time to get real with yourself, so it means a good amount of practice and patience. It can also be a tough process to go through alone, so there are some great exercises you can do to guide you through it.

One great way to engage in solo moments of introspection is through establishing a journaling practice. Journaling gives you a space to get things out of your head and into the ether. Whether by putting pen to paper or fingers to a keyboard (or screen), writing is one way to get to points of clarity about you and your processes. Sometimes this can look like pouring out a stream of consciousness, and other times prompts are helpful. If you're a fan of apps, there are some cool ones like Grid Diary or Jour. If you're more inclined to journal the old-school way, there are plenty of options out there that also offer thoughtful prompts. Or you can always act as your own guide by asking yourself questions such as:

- *What am I actually feeling right now?*

- *What might be informing some of the thoughts I'm having?*

- *What lens do I use when I'm looking at the world?*

- *What was driving me to act like that?*

Bringing your questions back to thoughts, feelings, and behaviors is always a great place to start, as these are the foundations to understanding how we operate and why. It can be really valuable to give yourself alone time or a soothing environment to help you get to an introspective mind space.

Of course, it's not necessary to be an introspection soloist. There's a reason orchestras have conductors: It's helpful to have someone directing you. There are people out there who are literally trained to help guide others in the process of looking at and understanding themselves. These fabulous humans are known as therapists. Though therapy is becoming more and more accepted as a regular ol' part of everyday life, stigmas are still alive and well. Some of the main ones include therapy patients being "weak" or "crazy," or the idea that there has to be something "wrong" with you to seek therapy. However, most therapists will affirm that it is much easier to prevent things than to fix them. In this way, therapy is a proactive part of self-understanding.

When You Don't Like
What You Find

. . . .

When taking care of your mind, you start tuning in to your mental and emotional well-being in new ways: mindfulness, journaling, one-on-one exploration, and more. This tuning-in can bring a sense of clarity, grounding, authenticity, and general good vibes. On the other hand, it can also stir up the tough stuff, like fear, anxiety, or sadness. Practicing regular introspection means being honest about the parts of yourself you might not be super proud of or the experiences you've had that have brought—and may continue to bring—painful emotions. When this happens, it is much easier to throw in the towel and say, *"Nope, too hard, too painful, not interested, see ya."* In this way, you start to lose momentum on making the changes you truly want to make. What's more, you can actually do more harm than good by ignoring the tough stuff. When you close yourself off to the stuff you don't like and only focus on the stuff you do, you aren't seeing yourself as a whole, only as bits and pieces. The truth is, everyone—and I mean *everyone*—has parts of themselves that are not so cute.

Ignoring the full spectrum of your feels ultimately makes adulting a hell of a lot harder than if you stay open to it. One way to stay open to the rougher bits is to really turn toward those who can guide you through them. Therapists are a major resource in this way. They are literally trained to help you both identify when you're actively in those tougher feelings and help you see their utility. Rather than shying away from the things that are hard, therapists guide their clients to lean into the tough stuff in a nonjudgmental way.

Taking Care of Your Body

There is no need to get religious to know the purpose behind the phrase "your body is a temple." Providing the body with care and consideration plays a major role in how you feel. When your body is run-down, overworked, overstuffed, or overtired, you lose your capacity for living as your best self. However, when you start to care for your body, you start to feel more energized from the inside. In the following pages, we'll look at three important ways to take extra good care of the beautiful vessel that is your body.

Cooking

How often do you choose ramen, cereal, or takeout for a meal instead of cooking? If your honest answer is "Pretty often," there's no shame in that game. It can be so much easier to get takeout or eat something microwavable. At the same time, cooking is a fabulous way to bring the focus back to you by giving your body some nutritious and delicious TLC. Also, when you've got a solid few recipes down, you can be impressive AF the next time you invite family, friends, or a date over. Aside from winning over those around you, cooking at home also brings some serious benefits.

Cost-Effective. Think about what you might spend when you go out to dinner. $15? $20? $30? $40? More? While shopping for groceries may feel pricey in the moment, those groceries will take you much further than a single meal out could. Your favorite dish from the restaurant down the street might cost $13 on its own (or more with tip). Re-creating that dish at home could easily cut the cost in half. By purchasing the ingredients yourself, you are also able to make that dish over and over again.

Control. A benefit of cooking at home is better control over getting what you want how you want it and when you want it. You can cater to your own dietary restrictions and specific desires at home. Not only will it be cheap to do, but it will taste awesome and offer you more nutritional value.

Fun. Cooking is a great way to get creative and try something new. It also pairs well with your favorite tunes and an impromptu dance party. Cooking doesn't have to only be about the biological need of satisfying hunger; it's also a great way to feed the soul.

Exercise

The great thing about taking care of your physical body is that it also has a positive effect on your mind. This win-win is commonly referred to as the mind-body connection. The mind-body connection is the scientifically proven interaction between mental and physical health. Engaging in physical exercise can help improve your mood and sleep, and decrease your overall stress. It's not a magic cure-all, but it definitely makes a difference. Why? Because your physical body has developed something called a stress-response cycle to respond to threats.

Your body doesn't know the difference between a terrifying animal charging at you and your siblings coming at you sideways. All it knows is that there's a threat and you better respond to it. The problem is that you can't run away whenever you have a stressful day at work or punch everyone who ever bothers you in the face. When that stress-response cycle is firing, all that energy has to go somewhere! One of the best places to put that energy is into a solid workout.

Workouts can take on many, *many* forms. When it comes to exercise, check in with your body and notice the types of movement that feel good. If you hate running, don't force yourself to run. If you're not quite sure where to start, give yourself the opportunity to try a smorgasbord of workouts. Lots of gyms or fitness classes offer free trials, making it easy to "gym hop" and experiment with different offerings until you find one that works for you. With so many available options, it can help to zero in on two broad types of exercise: cardio and strength. Getting in a mix of both is important, as they improve different parts of your physical health. Whether through dancing, cycling, weight lifting, Pilates, or organized sports, the key is to get your body moving. That movement is what helps complete those stress-response cycles and get you the physical *and* mental benefits that feel so great.

Moderation

When it comes to adulting, one big transition is from going hard to going medium. A totally natural part of being in your late teens and early twenties is feeling invincible. Part of that might be because your brain doesn't fully develop until you are well into your 20s, so you aren't the greatest at logic and reasoning. Another very real part is that your body can handle more during those years. You bounce back more quickly after pulling all-nighters, partying hard, or spending the day eating nothing but hot chips. Eventually, though, things start to catch up. Hangovers last longer, you feel less focused when you don't get enough sleep, and your body starts to feel sluggish when you aren't feeding it right. You simply can't go too hard for too long without struggling.

This isn't to suggest that you should shrivel into a husk of yourself by going to bed at 9:30 p.m. every night, always refusing a second round of drinks, and never eating chicken and waffles. Not at all! Life is all about balance. Balancing things out gives you the opportunity to live your life to the fullest without completely throttling your ability to thrive. There is frequency moderation, and there is quantity moderation. When you moderate how often you eat fried food, you are maintaining the pure pleasure of that activity. For example, you give yourself the ability to *really* enjoy those fries while still providing the nutrition your body needs at other times. When you moderate the amount of alcohol you drink at a friend's birthday party, you create the opportunity to enjoy the moment as intended without getting sloppy that night or feeling crappy the next day.

What's important here is that living a life of moderation doesn't have to be restrictive. Balance does not keep you confined or hold you back from the things you enjoy. It gives you the ability to both take great care of yourself *and* deepen your enjoyment of the things you like because balance implies that you don't constantly overdo those particular things.

How to Get through
the First Week of Change

When it comes to making lifestyle changes such as the ones talked about here, everyone struggles. This is a whole new path to walk down, and remembering to come back to this new path instead of the old ones takes a certain level of persistence and sense of investment.

If the labor required to make these changes is a "labor of should," as in "I *should* be cooking for myself," "I *should* be moving my body," or "I *should* be saying, 'No thanks,'" it's going to feel far more daunting. Do you really want to be doing any of these things if doing so means dragging your feet and cursing everyone and everything? On the other hand, if the labor required to make these changes is in fact a "labor of love," the experience is totally different, even when it's hard. Engaging in change as an act of self-love means willingness to put in the work. It's about choice—not force.

And, hey, even when change is coming from a place of love, it can still be a struggle. Here are some tips for making this change more doable:

Start small. Remember that there's no way you're going to overhaul your entire life in one go.

One thing at a time. You don't have to do all of the things at all of the times. Pick one chunk at a time to pour your attention into.

Employ the buddy system. Having a buddy by your side can help with accountability, and it also makes things way more fun.

Play. Don't forget to have fun! Per Disney, there's no reason you can't "whistle while you work."

Now, Revisit That List

After taking a look at the ways in which you can start focusing on you, it will be helpful to go back over that initial list of changes (page 17) in order to make adjustments. As you step further into self-prioritization, there may be things you want to shift around in order to continue to prioritize your wants, needs, and dreams as opposed to the wants, needs, and dreams of others. This gives you a chance to think more about how your list can include your mind and body.

The Art of Tough Love

As you start incorporating some of the things discussed in this book, notice the flavors of change taking place. You might notice a little voice pop into your head, pushing you to make your changes in a particular way. Even if the changes are authentic to your wants and needs, prioritize you, and sound awesome and exciting, there's a way in which you might end up putting heat on yourself to make it happen.

Figuring out the amount of heat you need and when you need it is not a science but an art—the art of tough love. It takes skill to know when to put the heat on and "tough love" yourself, and when to back off and provide some compassion instead. We all have a particular range in which we function best. In that range, there needs to be at least a little bit of pressure to light a fire under your booty. (If you want to get technical with it, I'm talking about the Yerkes-Dodson law, which tells us that to perform, we all need some physiological or mental arousal.) However, with too much pressure, you will end up not being a very happy camper, and you will not function nearly as well because you've freaked yourself out.

As you move through some of these changes, take stock of which ones you want to push harder on and which ones you'd rather back off of. When taking stock, don't forget that backing off, pressing pause, or stopping altogether is an act of self-compassion, *not* laziness. Folks seem to get caught up in the idea that extending compassion to yourself somehow makes you lazy. That can't be further from the truth. Dr. Kristen Neff notes that having compassion for yourself means understanding that painful things are going to exist, responding to that pain point by offering yourself warmth and caring instead of judgment, and remembering that pain is part of everyone's experience. So, don't leave out the love in tough love, and extend some kindness and compassion to yourself as you grow.

MY UPDATED LIST

Now, come back to the list of changes you want to make for yourself that you started in chapter 1. Take a gander at that sucker again and see what you notice. There could be changes on that list that you feel more committed than ever to making, or there might be things you're realizing don't matter to you as much. After taking the time to hang out with yourself and focus on you, does the original list still ring true? If there are bits you want to add or remove, go for it! If there are things you want to bump up to the front of the line or write out more clearly, heck yes! The lines below and on the following page are there for you to update to your heart's content.

_____

_____

_____

_____

_____

_____

_____

_____

_____

_____

Ready to Move Forward?

With your list further refined to reflect a focus on you, you are ready to go from engaging in a nifty little exercise to creating a legit *plan*. Then, with a plan rooted in prioritizing yourself, you are ready to transform it into action. It can feel overwhelming to move forward with things all at once, but don't trip! Putting a plan to action is as simple as one, two, three.

First, prioritize what's needed for *now*—not two weeks from now, not two months from now, not two years from now. Looking at your list, what can you use *right now*? Give that the spotlight for the time being.

Then, track your progress. One of the things you commonly hear about taking action is that you want to be able to measure it. The same way you want to know where you're starting in order to identify where you're going, you also want to be able to get a sense of how far you've gone. Whatever it is that you're prioritizing for now, track your progress with it. For example, did you notice that you've cooked three meals for yourself this week, compared to one last week?

Finally, adjust accordingly. So, you've prioritized the thing, and you've tracked your progress of the thing; now adjust if you need to. If you wanted to get introspective every day, but it doesn't seem to be happening, don't worry about it; you can tweak and fine-tune your game plan into whatever would make things more realistic for you (e.g., journaling two times a week instead of every day).

A Moment of Reflection

Now we are really getting our hands dirty with this adulting business. In this chapter we got real! Let's recap:

+ It is important to focus on yourself by prioritizing your own needs and knowing you're not doing anything wrong or bad by doing so.

+ There is great value in caring for your mind by understanding how to care for your mental and emotional health, stepping into an awareness of the present moment (aka mindfulness), and getting honest and introspective with yourself.

+ You can prioritize caring for your physical self by becoming your own personal chef, getting your body moving and shaking, and finding balance through moderation.

"Everybody needs somebody."

—Solomon Burke

CHAPTER THREE

Relationships (Because You Can Only Forget about Everyone Else for So Long)

Clearing away other people's opinions is no easy feat! Not only is looking inward tough work, but trying to ignore others while you do it is especially tough. None of us exist in a vacuum. Ultimately this is a good thing. If you lived in solitude, you'd drive yourself bonkers. People need people. Now that you've taken a moment to spend time with yourself, it's time to look outward again and reintegrate relationships with others back into your focus.

Family

Family relationships can be some of the stickiest and trickiest dynamics because they are where all of our relationship experiences typically begin. They are highly informative and very powerful because they shape our understanding of what it means to be in a relationship with other humans. Regardless of their quality, our familyships, be they loving, harsh, or somewhere in between, tend to stick with us in some way. Now, when we say *family*, we aren't simply talking about the people with whom we share genes. Family comes in all different flavors. When we use the words *family*, *parents*, or *siblings*, we are talking about anyone who had a strong hand in raising us and whomever we were raised with, regardless of biology. This means grandparents, aunties and uncles, cousins, friends, friends' parents, next-door neighbors, or whomever else might be considered family.

Evolving Relationships

Families are intricate systems with all sorts of nuance and complexity. The idiosyncrasies specific to our own family tend to come to the surface as we morph into our adult selves because our family relationships morph right along with us. We might relate to our caregivers in new ways that enlighten us or enrage us. We might see our siblings more as children or more as peers. As these relationships change, they can bring a whole boatload of feelings. There is no particular right (or wrong) way for our familyships to evolve. Regardless of how relationships shift, the truth is that any transition comes with some tension. Whether the tension is with a caregiver, a sibling, or oneself, it's a palpable force.

One of the best ways to navigate the tension underlying these transitions is to get out in front of it by naming it. Rather than let it sneak around under the surface, call it out. For example, if your younger brother finds his dream job before you've settled on what you want to be when you grow up, don't be afraid to have a conversation about your differences. If the subject is not mentally or emotionally safe enough to talk about with the person, sneak back into chapter 2, remember who your go-to guide is, and chat with them about it. The key here is giving the reality of the transitions a space to exist, whether that means laughing, crying, hoping, getting excited, getting curious, getting angry, or anything else in between.

Parents and Guardians

No matter the composition or dynamics of a family, there is a process that happens to each of us: the transition from being someone's child to being someone's adult-child. The relationships we have with our caregivers when we are young (often called "parent-child" relationships) usually have a particular power dynamic: The caregivers hold most of the power. They are the decision makers and enforcers. As we transition into adults, that power dynamic start to change. We start becoming our own decision makers, separate from our caregivers, and there's no fighting the fact that these transitions bring up some funky feels.

No matter how old you get, whoever raised you is going to see you as the person they are caring for. It doesn't matter if you're 15, 25, or 45. This is why you can't get too mad when your auntie still thinks she has a say in who you are dating or how late you stay out. Caregivers who previously played an active role in your life will continue to look out for you no matter how old you get. My 90-year-old Bubbie still tells my 60-something-year-old dad, "Don't do anything stupid." Even those who were less active in your upbringing may still see themselves as an authority due to the standard power dynamics between caregivers and children.

Where things get complex is the recognition that while you might still be someone's child, you are *also* a full-fledged adult human with autonomy and independence (aka the adult-child). What is especially challenging is the push-pull experience as you oscillate back and forth between wanting and needing your caregivers to chime in and not wanting or needing them to say anything. This is where flexibility becomes your best friend. As you grow into your early adulthood (and even beyond), give yourself the opportunity to move from the world of *either/or* to the one of *both/and*. You don't have to be either the adult or the child. You can absolutely have enough space to be both the adult and the child. One example of this might be sometimes reaching out to your mom for her guidance or opinion while at other times forging ahead and doing what you want to do in the way you want to do it.

Helicopter Parents

Growing up, did you have a caregiver who was very involved? I'm not talking about "dropped you off and picked you up from school" involved. I'm talking about "knowing the numbers of your teachers, the due dates for all of your projects, and every free throw you missed at your YMCA rec games" involved. Having a caregiver who is still hovering this closely can feel constricting—especially when you're trying to figure out life for yourself.

Before we knock anyone for being all up in your business, it's important to note that this flavor of caregiver typically wants you to both be awesome *and* feel awesome. For this reason, they might push you to do or share things in an attempt to keep you feeling safe, cared for, and confident. However, as you grow more fully into your adult self, all that nudging can get irksome. Start by getting curious. Talk to your person. When you can get to what's beneath all the pushing, you can better understand their motivation, as opposed to writing them off for being extra.

From there, boundaries kick in. Remember, boundaries are never punishment; they are the parameters you give yourself and others to keep everyone safe. When a parent starts to ask too many questions or give too many opinions, you get to set a boundary.

You might say to them:

"Hey, I appreciate you, but I've got this. I'll fill you in or ask for help when I'm ready."

Or say to yourself:

"I don't have to have all the answers to Dad's questions" or *"It's okay to not get her green light before I make decisions."*

These boundaries not only set you up to cultivate your loved one's trust in you, but they also prepare you to display your trust in yourself.

Parents Who Were Not Always Present

On the other end of the caregiver continuum are those who weren't quite so present and available. Sometimes these are caregivers who have trouble being there physically; other times they are caregivers who have trouble being there emotionally. For some, it can be a combo of the two. Like most complex experiences, this one can move you fluidly back and forth on the feelings spectrum. What is known for sure is that less available parents/caregivers can be tough to navigate, especially as you get older.

There are a host of situations that result in caregivers not being able to show up. Whatever the reason, the absence can result in some folks having a tougher time fulfilling their "parenting" duties. Whether you grew up with that flavor of caregiver or are currently experiencing it, an important piece of the puzzle is understanding that very rarely is a caregiver not present because of the child. In other words, it's not your fault. Does this make everything feel bright and shiny? No. But it can alleviate some of the painful questions of why a caregiver wasn't or isn't there.

As you grow into adulthood, you will want to share certain life events with a parent figure, like landing your first "real-world" job, falling in love, making a big move to a new city, celebrating holidays, having a crappy day, and many more. The challenge is traversing the sea of feelings these moments can stir up: sadness, anger, disappointment, regret, relief, and guilt, to name a few. Before trying to make sense of it all, know this: Whatever your response is to your experience, it's legit. So, whether it's through art, music, journaling, working out, dinner with friends, or therapy, give yourself the time and space to express yourself when you're feeling activated by their lack of presence.

Siblings

For the sake of simplicity, the term *siblings* will be used, but as stated earlier, a variety of people with whom you may have been raised might fit into this category regardless of genetics (cousins, friends, neighbors, and so on). Siblings are their own special type of family-ships as you transition to adulthood. Some particular challenges to sibling relationships can arise as you evolve into your grown self.

Comparing, Contrasting, and Competition. As you get older, "sibling rivalry" can come in the form of comparing yourself with your siblings and them comparing themselves with you. Physical looks, education, dating, careers, and everything in between can easily become points of comparison with the people with whom you were raised. Competing with your loved ones quickly gets in the way of giving and receiving support.

Leaving Someone Behind. As you start adulting, you might notice you feel less inclined to be with younger siblings with whom you'd typically connect. Adulthood tends to widen gaps and highlight differences between your journeys. It is easy to feel worlds apart once you graduate college, begin your career, or move out on your own. These gaps of leaving or getting left behind can strain a relationship.

Extending Your Family. Getting serious with a romantic partner means extending yourself beyond your own family system. As partners become serious, they become more like our family, which means they take up their own space within the system, usually at or near the top. This introduction of a new important relationship can feel threatening to siblingships.

Little Brothering (or Sistering or Cousining). This turn of phrase describes those moments that come up when, regardless of how old and adult you get, those power dynamics between younger and older siblings continue to exist. Similar to the way a caregiver will always see you as their child, it can be easy to always see or be seen as a younger sibling and treat or be treated as such. This can be an incredibly frustrating experience for whoever is placed on the downside of that power dynamic.

Roles and Responsibilities. When you are used to being irresponsible hooligans with the people you grew up around, one of the big transitions is around the roles and responsibilities within your family. Maybe you used to play the role of the clown, and now you're having to play the role of caretaker for your grandma. When you adult, you take on new or different responsibilities. This can bring challenges to your sibling relationships if they aren't used to you taking on a leadership role in family situations or vice versa.

Remember that as much as your siblings can be a pain in the ass, they can also be the best stress relievers, confidants, cheerleaders, and go-to people to lean on as the family dynamics shift. Don't forget what a resource they can be.

Friends

If there is one sentiment I hear repeatedly from the younger adults I work with, it is that making friends as an adult is *hard*. Yet at the same time, friendship is crucial to getting through life. Friends are often talked about as your "chosen family" for a reason. They are the ones who help hold you down and set you straight, the ones who can "tough love" you and "soft love" you, your ride-or-dies. That said, not all friendships are created equal. As you grow and evolve, so do your friendships and what you need from them. You might notice yourself becoming a bit more selective about whom you spend your time with. If guilt arises as a result, do your best to push it aside and come back to the importance of prioritizing your needs, one of which is solid friendships where you feel comfortable and safe.

Positive Friendships

When thinking about what makes a friendship legit, there are a few questions you can ask yourself.

"Do I Feel Seen?" Solid friendships are the ones in which you trust the other person to see you—really *see* you. They get excited about your awesome moments, hang out in your crappy ones, and support you in all your eccentricities. They are able to tune in to you and are pretty consistent about doing so. This doesn't mean that the friendships have to be all good vibes at all times, though.

"Can I Feel All My Feelings?" When you have a crappy day at work, feel super embarrassed after a weird date, are in the midst of a sad spell, or feel super proud of a major accomplishment, can you share that feeling with your friend(s)?

"Can I Be Honest?" Strong friendships are ones that make space for the good, the bad, *and* the ugly. They are the ones in which you can be honest. That means feeling comfortable saying yes or no, trusting that you can give and receive honest feedback, and being able to have the tougher conversations, like when your feelings get hurt.

Being seen, feeling your feelings, and being honest in a friendship are the foundations that help bring true growth into our lives. Also important is being able to move through those challenging moments that arise as friendships transition. Things like new partners, new jobs, or moving to new cities can make friendship difficult, but traversing those rough spots can make a positive friendship even stronger.

Positive friendships can enhance your well-being in all sorts of ways. For starters, one of our great needs as humans is a sense of belonging. When you build close friendships, that need gets met. You typically feel that you belong because you feel connected, and connection can both increase your self-esteem and reduce overall stress levels. Close friendships tend to promote your physical, mental, and emotional health by inviting you to grow. When those friendship foundations are met, friends are more likely to push you when you need to be pushed. Sometimes that can be through explicit efforts like making a pact to try a 30-day challenge together, but other times friendships push you implicitly. For example, when a friend disappoints you or lets you down, you are given the opportunity to grow emotionally by stepping into tough conversations and coming out the other side of them even stronger. All that said, friendship contributions are not a one-way street. In fact, if they were, you might notice the relationship feeling less than positive. Don't forget that as much as friends contribute to your growth, you also contribute to theirs. That means showing up for and challenging your friends, too.

The "Friends" You Were Warned About

Then there are the types of friends who don't seem to enhance your sense of well-being quite as much as you'd like them to. Throughout life, you will experience friends, and you will experience "friends." Either these air-quote friends aren't bringing you a whole lot of joy, or the goodness that comes with them is fairly inconsistent. If you find yourself answering "no" to one or all of the questions about being seen, feeling your feelings, and the ability to be honest, you might be identifying less than ideal "friends."

Many of us would much rather be in mediocre or even crappy friendships than be solo, which is understandable given how powerfully icky a feeling loneliness is. However, when you end up surrounded by less loving relationships, your overall sense of well-being plummets. Before learning how to navigate this flavor of friendship, you first have to be able to recognize it. Three signs to keep your eyes and ears open for are gossiping behind your back, put-downs, and general dismissal.

If you have a friend who regularly speaks negatively about you behind your back or tells stories about you that don't quite give the full picture, you might find it hard to feel safe and comfortable around them. Perhaps you can pinpoint various times when you have been made the butt of a joke. You might have been told things like *"Don't be so sensitive"* or *"Come on, I was just kidding."* Or you might struggle to share your honest opinion or experience with a friend because you find yourself being dismissed, pressured, or guilted. If any of these is true, this friendship might not be serving you. When you start to notice the ways in which some of your friendships are lacking, the big question is: *"Do I stay, or do I go?"*

If this is a friendship you want to keep and you are willing to put in the work to improve it, go for it! You'll need to get comfortable with uncomfortable conversations. You'll have to be honest with your friend about how you feel about their behavior and be real about your hurt feelings. Once the rupture has been brought out into the open, you and your friend can start the process of repair. Typically, this goes more smoothly when you are specific about what you need from them. Sometimes it's not enough to say, *"You really didn't show up for me when I needed you. Can you please try to show up more?"* Instead, ask specifically for what you need—for example, *"Hey, when I text you after a really hard day, it would be awesome if you could ask me more about what happened instead of just saying, 'Oh, that sucks.'"* Being specific gives you the opportunity to get what you need from the repair process; as opposed to getting the equivalent of a friendship Band-Aid, you can get a solid cast to hold the relationship as it heals.

On the other hand, if this is a friendship you're ready to release, I support the heck out of that, too! While romantic breakups seem to come with a clearer path, friend breakups prove to be much more challenging. Start by identifying the why:

- Have you naturally grown away from each other in terms of either general interests or differences in values?

- Has this friend become draining due to emotional dependence, toxicity, or competition?

- Are you hanging with this person purely out of feeling obligated to do so?

Answering questions like these can help you start to create a road map of understanding for yourself. Once you have a sense of *why*, you can start thinking about the *how*.

Oftentimes, people opt for the fade. It's tempting because it is the least confrontational and least likely to be awkward. The fading process is really about lessening the amount of interaction you have with a friend: less time spent together, fewer calls, fewer texts, fewer snaps, fewer hangouts. Phasing out a friendship is ideal when both people are in the same boat and each is fading out for their own reasons. While the fade can be a good fit for some, it can also drag things out and pose potential issues because you don't present your direct and clear intentions of stepping away from the friendship.

If this happens, you know it's time to get comfy with the discomfort and actually show up in order to step out. In other words, step into a conversation in order to step away from a friendship. Ideally, do this in person. As you prep for the conversation, come back to your *why* and turn it into your goal for your time spent with this person. Maybe you want to express pain points that have stayed with you, address a big miscommunication, or simply state the need for boundaries. The most important bit is to stick to *your* feelings as opposed to *their* friendship flaws.

Romantic Connections

So, you're a grown-ass adult, and after going on a whole bunch of dates (whether that's via Tinder, Hinge, Bumble, Animal Crossing, or—gasp—*IRL*), you find yourself partnered. Adulting in a romantic relationship definitely isn't child's play. However, it's important to acknowledge that for many people out there, the high school–style drama of relationships can continue regardless of age. Therefore, it is important to equip yourself with a solid toolbox that you can utilize to help you navigate romantic relationships in ways that are health-fueled instead of drama-fueled. Whether you are partnered for four months or four years, any relationship of any length is some-thing to learn and grow from. Doing so starts with the understanding that simply because a relationship ends does not make it a failure. You actually *want* your relationships to end. If they didn't, you'd still be entangled with the people you first attempted to date, which means you'd have very little insight about your wants and needs in the context of partnership. As you learn from your relationship experiences, you increase your ability to not only identify a more ideal fit for you but also be a more ideal fit for a future sweetheart.

Everyday Communication

In romantic relationships (and literally every other relationship), communication is key. Without it, there's no way you can derive a sense of pleasure, satisfaction, or fulfillment. What's more, without communication, you are quickly led down pathways that can cause a great deal of harm to yourself and others. When societal norms depict the idea of "happily ever after," it's easy to assume that a partner should "just know" what to do and how to do it. After all, isn't that what we see in movies and hear in love songs? What we don't see is the time, energy, effort, and discomfort that go into making relationships work. Unfortunately, relationship communication isn't a class you take in school. The good news is that with practice, it's actually fairly easy to learn and is one of those things that can really stick with you and become as natural as riding a bike.

Drs. John and Julie Gottman are bigwigs in the world of romantic relationships. With years and years of research to back them up, they've been super impactful in helping people learn how to more effectively communicate in their partnerships. When it comes to everyday communications, the Gottmans offer three skills to get really good at:

> **Turning Your Feels into Your Words.** When you first try to let someone know what's up, you have to find the right words for your feelings. This means becoming your own explorer and expanding your feelings vocabulary. This part is about communicating to your boo where *you* are at. This can take the form of completing a sentence as simple as, "I feel___." What this does is set the stage of *what* you are feeling before you even get into

how you came to feel that way. Then, of course, you can go into why you're feeling that way. Don't forget to stick to you and your experience (in other words, using "I" statements). You're speaking about you at this moment, not about your partner.

Help Your Person Do the Same. You can regularly invite your honey to do the same thing by getting curious about them. What do little kids do when they are curious? They ask tons of questions! *"How did it all go down?" "What was that like for you?"* and *"What do you feel like you need right now?"* are examples of questions you can ask to invite your partner to really express themselves to you in a way that gives you more insight into their experience.

Embody Empathy. When it comes to romantic relationships (and all relationships), empathy is one of the greatest tools in the toolbox. Empathy is not about feeling *for* the other person, but feeling *with* them. It's the way we let our loves know that they are not alone and that what they are feeling is valid. Some empathic statements you can try out include *"No wonder you were so pissed," "That sounds terrifying," "Oh man, that must have sucked,"* or *"That definitely makes sense."*

These communication skills don't have to happen in any particular order for them to be super useful day to day. They also don't exist as a one-way street. If your partner isn't putting their feelings into words, getting curious about your feelings, or offering up some empathy, you can share these lovely communication skills and ask your significant other to practice using them with you.

How to Make Space for Someone New

When you start dating with a more serious intention, you are forced to learn how to make space for someone new. At the same time, you have to start thinking about how to continue to occupy space and stand in your truth. This dance of finding the right balance between yourself and a potential bae is all part of dating like an adult. When people talk about dating, the language that often gets used is that of "playing games." When you find yourself ready to date for real, that means being ready to step away from the "games." Rather than leaving someone "on read," getting possessive about whom you're "talking" to, or being noncommittal, it's time to step into actions that exemplify those very important traits of curiosity, self-awareness, and mindfulness. These are the foundational pillars of healthy dating.

In real life, these traits look like knowing what you want and desire and then communicating openly with dates about it. By doing so, you are better able to avoid those moments of "playing games" such as saying yes to a date when you're not actually into it or even straight-up ghosting. At the same time, these traits also mean understanding that you are not responsible for fixing someone's hurt feelings after saying "no thank you" to their advances or invitations.

Dating is certainly not for the faint of heart because it pushes you to get real with yourself and others. It's easy to get discouraged, but true growth never came from sitting still. As you learn to make space for a romantic partner, you will fumble and bumble through it a few times; that's a fact. What matters is that you stay curious and continue evolving.

Conflict Is Healthy

In a romantic partnership, or any relationship for that matter, fighting doesn't have to mean going 12 rounds of a back-and-forth screaming match and leaving each other's egos and hearts bruised. In fact, if arguments with your honey could easily start out with Michael Buffer bellowing, "Let's get ready to rummmmmbbbllle," it's time for some new skills. See what happens when instead you understand your "fight" as a disagreement, clash, or quarrel. Navigating arguments with someone through a lens other than "fighting" allows space for more intimate experiences, like vulnerability. The trick to relationship conflict is twofold: knowing when to step in and knowing when to step out. No matter how evolved and skilled you are, conflict is an unavoidable part of being in relationships with another person (romantic and otherwise).

Unfortunately, schools don't typically teach how to engage in conflict, especially with romantic partners. Many people have even been taught to do the opposite by being encouraged not to "rock the boat." Maybe in your family system, conflict came with physical, mental, or emotional harm. Or maybe you learned that everything needs to be all smiles all the time, and that if it's not, you're doing something wrong. When you receive messages like these, it's easy to see conflict as scary, bad, and something to avoid. The truth of the matter is that conflict is both inevitable and an opportunity for growth. Stepping into conflict means stepping into the chance to learn about yourself, your partner, and your relationship.

As important as it is to be able to move toward the rockiness of conflict in relationships, it is equally important to know when to back off and find more solid footing. If you notice voices rising, tones starting to sting, and language getting harsh, give yourself the gift of calling a time-out. Time-outs seem almost too easy, but think about it: In any sport, what happens when a time-out is called? Each player (or team) takes a step back to recalibrate and find a better game plan. Then— and this is the most important part—they *return* to the game. Taking a time-out in an argument with your partner doesn't mean storming out and calling it quits. It means pressing pause and taking a little time to get grounded before coming back to each other to continue discussing the issue at hand. Healthy conflict in romantic relationships is all about giving and receiving respect.

Showing and Receiving Love and Respect

R-E-S-P-E-C-T. Find out what it means to *you* (and your boo). Being in a romantic relationship (or any relationship) means doing the dance of both giving and receiving respect. To do this dance, you need to be able to recognize the steps and how to maneuver back and forth with them. That means having a solid sense of what respect is and what it is not. Before you get into the fancy footwork, start with the recognition that you and your partner are whole humans. This means you're not only dating the parts of them that are super enjoyable and vice versa. Recognizing each other as whole means acknowledging and honoring that there will be differences in thoughts, feels, experiences, and opinions. Respect comes in when you move beyond acknowledgment and step into a loving acceptance that these differences not only are present but are totally okay.

Does your partner know what your values are? Do you know theirs? If you value authenticity and they value humility, how do you work together to make space for each other's values? If you notice yourself having some trouble answering these questions, don't trip. Looking at, identifying, and talking about values actually makes for a really awesome date-night activity. The glorious thing about values is that there is no wrong way to do them. They don't fall into any potential traps of being good or bad, right or wrong. You can't really fight about them because all values are valid values. And validation is the fertile soil from which respect grows.

Historically, you may have received the messaging, whether explicitly or implicitly, that love and respect are immediate when you enter romantic partnerships. What gets left out are the ways in which that love and respect are earned. You and a potential partner start earning each other's love and respect from the moment you start engaging. This is when you should be on the lookout for feeling validated by your partner *and* when you should start providing that validation to them as well. When you feel validated in your experiences, you can better engage wholeheartedly in trust, communication, space (yes, time apart for each other is a necessary thing), negotiation, reliability, and open differences. When there is a lack of validation, there is a lack of respect. And when there is a lack of respect, there is a lack of love. This is when you are more likely to shy away from your partner and they from you.

When validation is actively happening, you'll notice yourself feeling particularly heard, seen, understood, or hopefully all of the above! In the day-to-day of your busy lives, this is as simple as staying present when telling each other about your days. But even more, it's stepping into each other's worlds to see from each other's points of view. This process is how you two show each other that you accept each other as is. This doesn't mean never challenging or questioning each other. It simply means doing so from a place that continues to legitimize each other. After all, aren't we all aiming to be too legit to quit?

A Moment of Reflection

This chapter came chock-full of all the different ships we sail in our daily lives: caregiverships, siblingships, friendships, and romantic partnerships. The relationships in our lives are powerful AF. Here's what we know:

+ Family relationships with our caregivers and siblings really transition when we start adulting. A shift is required from seeing you as a kid to seeing you as an adult. This shift in perspective can be tough, so boundaries are your friend here.

+ Friendships can either keep you afloat or drag you under, and it's up to you to keep your eyes and ears open for signs they are not serving you. Sometimes a friendship is ripe for repair, and other times you can find a way to let it go.

+ Romantic relationships take work—communicating, navigating conflict, and showing and receiving respect. The crux of this work is showing love for your partner by validating them and feeling validated by them in return.

The Basics, Covered as Painlessly as Possible

Going over the basics can feel like one big eye roll. I swear, if one more person talks about learning how to change a tire…But even if none of us wants to admit it, a lot of these basics truly are necessary. So, this book includes some quick tips, assembled together in an interesting way to make them slightly more intriguing.

Don't forget, we all have different life experiences. If this section or something in it doesn't quite apply to you, feel free to move right past it!

DOMESTIC STUFF

- Be realistic about rent. You probably won't find your "dream" apartment on a budget, so get real about what will work for you for now.

- Not everyone has to be your best friend, and even those we like the most can be tough to live with. With roommates, name your negotiables and nonnegotiables while knowing there will always be compromise.

- Cleaning sucks, but it's way easier to do in small spurts. Try not to let things go for months without a clean. If you're wiping down counters or vacuuming here and there, cleaning will be far less daunting.

- Pets are no-joke responsibilities and can be costly. If you're craving a four-legged friend, ask yourself if you're ready to care for it the way it deserves.

- Save your money and go light on the Ubers. Learn the buses, trains, trolleys, and shuttles in your area. They are less expensive and also support the community you live in.

HYGIENE AND WARDROBE

- Showering, flossing and brushing, and deodorant are the top three hygiene necessities. Don't be that person making others uncomfortable with your funk.

- Aside from maintaining your everyday personal hygiene, make sure you are staying up-to-date with your physical health by scheduling yearly physicals, regular STI screenings, and Pap smears if you are the proud owner of a vagina.

- For work attire, start by identifying a go-to interview outfit and build from there. In most cases, this means going business casual (but it pays to do your research on the company and corporate culture just in case). This means slacks/khakis; a collared shirt, blouse, or sweater; and dress shoes.

- Updating your look every now and then doesn't have to break the bank. Check out thrift and discount stores in person and online (e.g., ThredUP and Poshmark). Of course, there are always sales to keep your eyes peeled for!

THE POWER OF YOUR VOICE

- The service industry is not the entitlement industry. When people are working hard to take care of the needs of others, it is imperative to speak with kindness and gratitude.

- Don't be afraid to speak up, either when things don't feel right or when they feel super right. Practice naming the tough stuff *and* the awesome stuff.

- There are definitely times to open your ears instead of your mouth. This can be when there are lessons to be learned or when other voices need to be heard more than yours does. Don't forget to help raise the voices around you.

- Don't write like you text. Abbrevs (see what I did there) are cool. However, try to be mindful of using full sentences and punctuation when composing texts/emails/snail mail to family, colleagues, or friends.

SOCIAL MEDIA

- Text your heart out, but don't forget the importance of in-person chats. Take the time to decipher what flavor of conversation is best saved for face-to-face—or at least voice-to-voice.

- Sexting… Bet you never thought you'd read someone telling you to go for it, huh? Well, this is me telling you to go for it. *However,* this is also where I tell you to be smart, courteous, mindful, consenting, and well informed of potential consequences.

- As with most things in life, too much of a good thing can totally become a…thing. Don't forget to give yourself digital breaks.

- One of the great things that tech has to offer is online dating. Though conversation may start online, don't forget that you're talking to (and are) a person, not a bot. Extend the same cautions and courtesies that you would for dating offline.

FREE STUFF AND SCAMS

- One way for companies to up their sales is to offer free delivery. Those new Air Jordans or that pad thai can look *extra* tempting when you know it will be delivered for free. Don't forget to first ask yourself, *"Have I paid all my bills yet?"*

- Heck yeah, try out all those free skips on Pandora or Spotify, but don't forget to cancel that subscription unless you're prepared to start paying. If you sign up for something for free, set a reminder to unsubscribe before the free trial ends.

- Recently, cell phone providers have been providing alerts for "telemarketer" or "potential spam." You can totally pick up the phone, or, of course, you can let a number you don't recognize go to voicemail.

- If you receive a questionable email, even from a name that you recognize, double-check the sender's email address. If your Uncle Gustavo's email is not pingumz395@legit.mail, it might be a scam.

- When connecting with someone online (dating or otherwise), do your due diligence to get a sense of who they actually are. Google searches aren't a bad place to start.

BABY STEPS TO BECOMING MORE AWARE OF THE WORLD

- Identify a reputable news source that gives you a basic briefing in order to stay up-to-date without becoming overwhelmed. Staying informed is important, but being inundated by the 24-hour news cycle can be detrimental.

- Take the steps to hear other thoughts, feels, and views. It's easy to surround yourself with like-minded people. However, too much of the same can also hinder your growth. Get curious about people, places, things, and ideas that differ from you/yours.

- Local government is an awesome way to truly establish a sense of feeling rooted in and connected to your community. Check out who your local representatives are, and see what they do for your neighborhood.

- There's no clearer way to say it: *Your. Vote. Matters.* Exercising citizenship is an awesome privilege. Get out there and rock the vote!

"What have I learned about life? . . .
Learn to get along with jerks—it's difficult."

—George A. Caravalho

CHAPTER FOUR

How to Kill It at Work

Work, work, work, work, work, work. You might not be able to hear it in your head, but Rihanna is playing because this chapter is all about that grind—the daily work grind. The one that sometimes comes with drinking copious amounts of coffee as you try to recognize your passion and filter it into something you can do day in and day out. The grind that invites you to get excited about what's working and get mad about what's not. This chapter is here to help you slay through it all.

Making It Matter

Let's jump right into the real-talk deep end: Forcing yourself to "find your passion" is BS. Gasp! Hold on a second before chucking this book across the room and let me explain. There are a few important pieces to this puzzle. A small chunk of folks out there *know* what they're passionate about. Somewhere within them is an energy or vibe or general excitement that "calls" to them, like the sea to Moana or basketball to Steph Curry. If you happen to be one of those folks who feel called to a particular thing, then keep on keeping on! Whether that thing is as concrete as a deep love of cross-stitch or more abstract like really being a leader, you do you by heeding the call.

However, if your honest-to-goodness answer to the question *"What's your passion?"* is *"I have no freaking idea,"* there isn't anything wrong with that. In fact, it's the more common answer. Having a fire lit in your belly about something and then getting to actually do that thing is freaking awesome. But here's where the logic of pushing everyone to find their "thing" is flawed: It creates a lot of pressure and, more often than not, assumes an obsessive sort of fixation that's not always true to life.

Let's look at the language for a moment. This is another one of those tricky bits, like self-focus, that has been lumped in with a whole bunch of underlying assumptions. The first of these is that passions are fixed in some way. If this idea is true, it suggests that once you've chosen a path to follow, especially if that path was chosen based on a passion, then you're not allowed to change your mind. However, not being able to change your mind means not being able to adjust. And not being able to adjust means not being able to grow and evolve. Start by giving yourself the freedom to adjust accordingly.

A second underlying assumption is the suggestion that your passion should be turned into a career that you eat, sleep, and breathe. For some, the answer might feel like a yes. Yes, I do want cross-stitch to be the thing that becomes my daily grind because it feels that big to me. If that's the case, then you can start thinking about how to get that grind going. However, for many people, passions don't necessarily have to turn into careers or be tied to work (aka money). If you grew up around cars and have loved getting to know their ins and outs, you might find yourself wide-eyed with excitement at the opportunity to fix up a 1965 Mustang. However, you might not actually want your daily grind to be all classic cars, all the time. Instead, your day-to-day work might be something that you enjoy well enough and that provides you the resources and flexibility you need to really enjoy this passion.

The next big assumption that gets lumped into the pressure to find your passion is that if you find it and make it your work, you will wake up every day with a smile on your face, jazzed to go to work, feel completely fulfilled by it, and never want to do anything else. I am here to tell you that this is simply not reality. No matter how much someone likes their job, there will be days when the job is total crap. Days when you can't fathom having to look at another email, send another invoice, or wire another lighting fixture. This is a universal life truth; at one point or another, things will suck. This is not meant to freak you out but to give you a realistic sense to help drive you toward greater clarity.

With the understanding that sometimes you're going to be unenthused by work (even if it's your dream job), you'll have an easier time finding the thing you're most willing to do. In other words, the real question you want to ask yourself is not *"What's my passion?"* but rather, *"How can I spend my time doing something that matters to me?"* Of course, that means identifying what matters to you in the first place. You might be thinking to yourself, *"Oh great, another thing that I have to figure out."* Well, I've got great news for you…you've already identified what matters to you. Back in chapter 2, you glanced at a list of values provided in the back of the book. Take a look at that list again and bring to mind the ones that stood out. Got 'em? Good! Values are the things that matter to you. Leaning into work that is rooted in your values means keeping your eyes peeled for possibilities and opportunities that feel meaningful to you. It also increases the likelihood that you'll see openings in challenging situations rather than feeling completely discouraged. When you look back at those values, see if you can spot any of them in previous jobs you've had. College jobs, high school jobs, volunteer gigs, whatever it may be, notice the times when you felt most useful and engaged. Which of your values was present?

Finding a work path to walk down does not necessarily have to be about passion but can absolutely be about what you find meaningful. This is a great way to start thinking about what you have to offer that the world might be in need of. While your passions might change or work might stink, your values will remain relatively constant. Your *values* are what make up your own personal compass to follow.

Take What Matters, and Apply It to Work

The notions of finding your "passion," "calling," or "life's purpose" comes with a lot of baggage. Instead, questions like "What matters to me?" "What feels important?" and "What do I value?" give you the chance to have a fuller picture that's not so pressurized. The kicker is to take what matters to you and bring it with you when you go to work. Bringing your values with you to work is no different than bringing your shoes. Unless your work is stomping on grapes to make wine or monitoring a bounce house, you probably wear shoes every day. In fact, I would venture to say that you rarely leave home without them. Values should be the same way: something you rarely leave your home without.

As you start to really think about the work you're either currently doing or want to do, take note of where and how your values fit in. For example, let's say that one of the things that really matters the most to you is authenticity. To you, this means being able to be yourself no matter where you are, what you're doing, or whom you're talking to. It also means other people getting to do the same. What sort of work could you imagine doing that would create the space for a value like this one? As the owner of a business, you'd get to be the one calling the shots and setting the tone for how you and others get to show up to work. As a stand-up comedian, you'd get to use authenticity as material for your act. If authenticity is a guiding value for you and you don't feel like you are getting to be yourself as an office manager or schoolteacher, you might notice the ways in which getting up and going to work doesn't sound all that appealing to you.

It's not absolutely necessary (or possible) to be head over heels in love with your job at all times, but since work is where adults spend a solid chunk of their time, it's worthwhile to assess what's necessary for engaging in work that feels interesting and important enough to not make you want to gouge your eyeballs out. Once you have your values on lock, there are a couple of things to consider in order to start to identify a potential work path that you might enjoy…at least until you are ready for a shift, because don't forget: It's okay to change your mind about your job.

First, ask yourself what you're good at. No matter how values-aligned something is, it's hard to enjoy the day in, day out of a job if you don't ever feel a sense of competency. You might really value showing up as your most authentic self, but if fine motor skills aren't exactly in your wheelhouse, then cosmetology might not be the direction for you. However, if you are a whiz when it comes to Excel, budgeting, and overall money management, you may really enjoy bookkeeping for salons or individual hair and makeup artists. There are concrete and abstract things to be good at—for example, coding (concrete) and empathy (abstract). Take note of your different skills and the values they embody.

Next, ask yourself where the money is. On its surface, a question like this can sound a lot like greed, yet you've got to find a way to pay your bills, and the getting paid piece is what turns the values and skills into a job. Otherwise, it's more of a hobby, which is still an awesome thing and sometimes makes more sense. Not everyone wants or needs to turn their hobbies into their careers. To make that cheddar, there are typically two avenues:

1. Identify what opportunities exist that allow you to exercise your skill(s) and your value(s).

2. Determine where there might be a gap in current opportunities and make something new to fill it.

Although the second option is totally doable, the path can be pretty gnarly and one that most of us don't walk down immediately due to the incredible amount of time, energy, and resources it takes. So, for the time being, concentrate on the first option because there are tons of ways to apply your values and your strengths to a job. Whether you're super handy at fixing things up around the house, love cooking and feeding others, or are an incredible planner for all kinds of get-togethers, there's likely something out there that's right up your alley. What comes next is figuring out what to do once you get there.

Recognize and Respect Your Work's Existing Culture

Whether you've landed a gig that aligns with your values and gives you the opportunity to engage in work that feels important to you or you are still working to identify the right career, you will still be navigating your work's culture. As you step into the body shop, the office, the classroom, the restaurant, the Zoom meeting, or wherever you do your job, start to notice vibes around you. Workplace culture is made up of a number of things, including people, leadership, mission, and general workplace practices. What follows are a few different ways that you can start to really dive into that culture.

Networking

Networking is a word that gets tossed around a lot when it comes to the workforce. It's so much more than plastering on a fake smile to shake hands with people over lukewarm coffee and dried-out pastries. Networking is about connecting with other people who both are and are not like you. The exciting similarities come from getting to nerd out with people who are just as into the work as you are. The intriguing differences come from getting to learn about other angles or values in your industry because, of course, there's no one right way to go about things. When you network, you are weaving yourself into the cultural web of people and information that will boost your ability to grow.

Finding a Mentor

One of the awesome things that can come out of networking and weaving into your work culture web is the potential to find a mentor. In some fields, mentorship is sort of built in, such as through apprenticeship or particular supervision practices. However, your particular workplace might not come with that opportunity. Mentorship is about establishing a connection to someone from whom you can really learn. While mentors can be bosses, they don't have to be. In fact, some people prefer to have mentorship from people within their field but outside their workplace.

Mentors are trusted advisors who can really show you the ropes as you're getting started and can continue to guide you as you grow. As you move along your work path, take stock of those around you, either actually at work or in your networks. Is there anyone whose accomplishments you admire or who you might want to emulate some day? Anyone whose values appear to align with yours or whose way of being you appreciate? The best mentors are often the ones we become giddy about not only because they've done great things but also because they've done them in ways that feel noble or honorable. Finding a mentor is a great time to check back in with your values.

Create New Initiatives

Hopefully by now it doesn't shock you to hear that nothing's perfect. No matter how values-aligned and important and fabulous and awesome your job is, there are still going to be some cracks. The great news is you can be the person who not only identifies a crack but helps patch it up. When an aspect of your work culture is lacking and you have an idea for improvement, a new initiative is born. Creating new initiatives doesn't mean walking into work throwing bows by redlining policies and nitpicking procedures. It's more about taking note of important gaps and offering suggestions to close them.

For example, if you notice your workplace looks a little homogenous, you might be inclined to spearhead a diversity, equity, and inclusion (DEI) committee that focuses on representation. Implementing new ideas means you have to start by presenting them. If they stay in your head, there's no way that gap is going to get filled. Begin by coming up with a proposal that describes what you want to do, why you want to do it, how you hope to do it, and what you'll need to get it done. Even if it's something as simple as a coffee machine in the back office to help make sure you and your fellow technicians stay properly caffeinated, you can step into your work culture by stepping into your voice.

Bring Forth the Professional You

Speaking of your voice, coming into a work culture also means coming into your own as a professional. Regardless of how formal or informal your work culture is, there is still a work-life version of you that is at least a little bit different from the personal-life version of you. That said, authenticity—getting to be your true self regardless of where you are or whom you're around—matters. When thinking about where you currently work or where you'd like to work, there will be parts of your authentic self that get to stand center stage and others that will have to exit stage left. This doesn't mean ignoring who you are; it simply means knowing your audience. If your personal authentic self might curse like a sailor when excited, your professional authentic self might take the potty mouth out of the picture while keeping the rambunctious bits intact. As you tap into the culture of a workplace, you will get a sense for how you want to show up as your most professional self. However you show up, don't forget to make sure it's in line not only with the culture being brought to you but also with the values you bring to the culture.

Learn to Play the Game

As much of a bummer as learning to "play the game" is, it's part of being in the workforce. No matter how much the idea of playing games makes you shudder, that subtle (or not-so-subtle) thing known as "office politics" is real. As nice as it would be to be totally indifferent to workplace politics, they directly impact you, your coworkers, and the work itself. Rather than ignore office politics, face them head-on. This section will give you some guidance on how to navigate them.

Politics is a word that can make hairs stand up, shoulders tense, and skin crawl. But not all politics are the kind that make you sell your soul. Values, remember? In fact, learning to play the game is another way you can really weave yourself into your workplace culture because politics are a big part of that webbing. At the core are your relationships and the sincerity with which you approach them. For example, if you're teaching second graders, and, as cute as they are, you'd rather focus on making the school awesome instead of making only your classroom awesome, you may need to do some maneuvering.

In order to maneuver smoothly:

- Be perceptive of where others are at. You will have to meet your workplace culture and colleagues where they are as opposed to where you want them to be.

- Positively influence those around you and excite change.

- Have an additional network of support to help make things happen.

Then, of course, make sure folks truly experience you as sincere in your desire to improve the work culture as a whole. If you're looking to level up, this is the kind of stuff that can help get you there.

When It Doesn't Feel Right

Not everyone is constantly looking to level up, and even for those who do want to make those kinds of moves, playing the office politics game can feel all kinds of wrong. The negative vibes of "bad politics" are pretty hard to miss. They can be as abstract as a tight and uncomfortable feeling in your gut or as concrete as getting an earful of gossip every time you show up for your shift. Oftentimes, you might experience a combo of internal and external symptoms. When the culture you're in invites you to play games that cause harm to yourself, others, or the organization as a whole, don't be afraid to recognize the situation for what it is. If you feel like you have to do things that are misaligned with your values, take note.

If there are some negative sides to the culture of your work, feel free to smile and wave as that negativity train rolls right on by. There are going to be parts of your work that you're not a huge fan of. For example, you might love the restaurant industry. Hosting, serving, managing, cooking, and being around food aligns with your value of nurturing and feels important enough to you that you want to engage in it on the daily. However, sometimes the restaurant business can be a whole lot like rock-and-roll without the music. If you're not down to bond with your owner by staying late after closing and having a few beers, let that train leave the station. Do you by staying committed to your values.

A Note about Not Getting Discouraged

Playing the game of workplace politics can feel like being pressured to "sell your soul." You might find it easier to simply stay out of the drama. Unfortunately, there's no avoiding it entirely because, as stated previously, these implicit dynamics are part of that complex work culture web. You can, of course, do your very best to RSVP "no" to things like gossip and cliques, but when there's no true escaping workplace politics, there are a few ways to keep from getting totally discouraged.

Take the Role of Observer. This is a great way to sit back and take note of the goings-on around you without having to feel stuck in the middle of them. As an observer, you can simply ask questions, either to yourself or to others, without having to take any particular action. Giving yourself the time and space to observe gives you the chance to get a fuller understanding of your work environment.

Remember the Buddy System. Because the idea of playing the game can automatically make some people feel like they have to put their guard up, it can help to know whom you can lean on and talk candidly with about your observations.

Be Your Own Compass. If you're noticing funky dynamics such as power struggles or less-than-fair rulings, come back to your values. If you're needing an external compass, former First Lady Michelle Obama gave us all the great adage, *"When they go low, we go high."*

Decide When Enough Is Enough. Each person has a different tolerance level. When you've reached capacity and know there's not enough wiggle room to turn things around, empower yourself with the autonomy and freedom to gracefully make your exit.

"Fake It 'til You Make It"

There are pros and cons to this age-old saying. It encourages you to explore and experiment a bit. You don't have to know everything from the get-go, and one of the best ways to learn is by doing. Imposter syndrome is a very real experience that I work with often. Part of adulting at work is getting comfortable with the uncomfortable feelings when taking the reins, even when you feel like you don't have the same gravitas as those who have been around longer than you have. One big pro of the "fake it 'til you make it" sentiment is the way in which it urges you to trust yourself. When you're thinking, "What the hell am I doing?" or, "How the hell did I get here?" trust that you both deserve to be where you're at and can totally figure out whatever comes your way.

However, this philosophy can come with the underlying suggestion to not ask for help when you need it—to pretend you've "got it" even when you don't. This is messaging you want to push back against. When you're confused, floundering, unsure, or just plain lost, reach out! Bosses, coworkers, and mentors are all there to help you learn the ropes and make it through. At the same time, don't forget that you've also got a big brain between those ears and definitely have what it takes to make it!

How to Handle Your Job When It Isn't What You Thought It Would Be

We've all been there: You walk in on your first day, bright-eyed and bushy-tailed, ready to slay. Then as you go, the slaying becomes a little more difficult because more things turn into dragons. Maybe it's your boss or a coworker, or maybe a project you were working super hard on tanks. Sometimes, you can slay those dragons as they arise. Sometimes, there are too many of them to slay and the decision to stay or go has to be made. While it doesn't always feel fantastic in the moment, learning how to navigate the tougher stuff at work is just as important as (if not more so than) learning how to kick ass and take names. In fact, you can't really do one without the other.

How to Have Awkward and Difficult Conversations with Your Boss

Whether you want to ask for a promotion, talk about trying your hand at something new, or give some critical feedback, conversations with head honchos can be tough to stomach. Regardless of what you're bringing to the boss, there are a handful of things to keep in mind to help those chats go a bit more smoothly.

Keep It in Person, Keep It Private, and Keep It at Work.
I know, I know, it would be *so* much easier if this could be handled in an email. However, if you want to make sure to be heard, it's got to happen in person. You also want to make sure to get your boss's undivided attention, so in the office kitchen or at a company happy hour might not be the most ideal space. Find a private space at work to make sure the conversation gets the focus it deserves.

If You're Bringing up an Issue, Also Bring up a Solution.
If you're coming to your manager with something that doesn't work so well, help yourself out by bringing with you an idea or two of how you imagine adjusting things. This automatically turns the conversation into a collaboration.

Stay Accountable. Difficult conversations are only made more challenging when you attempt to remove yourself from them. Be sure to make note of your contributions and responsibilities in any situations that arise.

Leave Guilt at the Door. Thoughts like "It's not that big a deal" or "It's fine" or "I'm making too much noise" can be dropped into a box outside the shop, office, or restaurant. Having these convos with your boss is a literal part of their job description. Inviting them to do their job is nothing to feel guilty about, especially if doing so means meeting your needs as an employee.

How to Deal with Your Coworkers

Though work doesn't need to be a sitcom, sometimes it can feel like one with all the different characters you encounter. You could meet some of your greatest lifelong friends or even romantic partners through work, and you could also run into a few of these along the way:

The Negative Nellies and Neds. If you notice a coworker who is a bummer to be around, you might have one of these on your hands. They are tough because while they might get pumped on the negative vibes, they can totally drain you. Some of your response options are to listen quietly (rather than actively engage the negativity), excuse yourself from the conversation, or gently name the negative and invite a redirection toward a more supportive stance.

The Constant Competitor. While friendly competition can help boost your work drive, some folks can easily forget that you're not in the Olympics vying for a gold medal. More often than not, we want to be in collaboration with our coworkers as opposed to competition. You can invite a competitive coworker to collaborate with you. If you don't quite trust them to not throw down the gauntlet, then give yourself the space to focus on doing you. Your best is all you or your bosses can ask for.

The Village Yenta. *Yenta* is the Yiddish word for "gossip" or "busybody," and every village has its yenta. When you're spending this much time with a group of people, stories are bound to go around. This person might enjoy being the giver and receiver of those juicy deets. In response to these folks, you may want to (a) steer clear of providing them with your intimate thoughts and feels, and (b) express indifference to their attempts to share the latest "hot goss" with you.

The Slackers. Everyone needs a bone thrown to them now and then, but when you notice a coworker not carrying their own weight, it can get real frustrating, real fast. To nip this situation in the bud, take a direct approach by asking them to step up their game or letting them know that you won't be able to keep covering their shifts.

How to Handle Yourself When Projects Go South

Sometimes you are going to absolutely slay the thing you have been working on, and other times things are going to fall flat. That's simply the nature of the game. Whether it's a boring lesson plan, an engine you can't quite get a handle on, or a PowerPoint presentation that doesn't quite land, flubs are going to happen. Handling these moments is not about how to best engage in self-flagellation but about engaging in the opportunity to learn and grow.

In the profound words of Vanilla Ice: *"Stop! Collaborate and listen."* These four words are genius for responding to project struggles. First is the stopping. Knowing to either press pause on something that isn't working or stop listening to all the thoughts swirling around in your head after a project has already stopped working is major. You then have an opportunity to take a beat to breathe and step back from the weeds you may have gotten into.

Next, figure out what isn't working or why something didn't work. To do this, you'll need to collaborate and listen to feedback and input. Whether that feedback is from people or data, seek out the information you need. This is a great opportunity to not only find out more about what's going wrong but also learn about what's going right and how to keep that momentum moving. A big piece of this puzzle is staying in a growth mindset. When you start to get down on yourself, you can quickly spiral into all the reasons you suck. Screw that! You don't suck, you slay, and flubs are an important part of kicking ass and taking names.

How to Know When to Stay and When to Go

When you start to take note of things not feeling quite right at work, you eventually have to ask yourself the big question: *"Should I stay, or should I go?"* It is not an easy decision to make and often comes with a lot of complexity. At the end of the day, it's about doing what's right for you at any given moment. And there's no shame in that game. Ever.

What It Means to Stay

There are a slew of reasons to stay at a job that isn't the brightest, shiniest, most exciting, feel-good thing in the world. It might sound disheartening, but plenty of folks decide that staying put in a job they don't love is the best decision for them.

The Money. If where you're at pays the bills *and* gives you the opportunity to save, it could be a worthwhile investment to stay put while you build up that savings account.

The Future. Another common reason to hang on is for a bright, shiny future. You might not like the work itself, but the organization, the people, or the mission might be killer. Sometimes it's worth trudging through the mud if doing so gets you to other places you're trying to go.

The Résumé. It is completely legitimate to stay in a particular position for the purpose of building that skill set or having that particular company on your résumé.

Yet sometimes the money, people, or growth simply won't be enough, and you'll decide to pack your bags and go.

When and How to Exit Gracefully

Regardless of your reason for leaving the job, quitting isn't always the easiest thing to do. As with making the decision to stay, deciding to leave and then acting on that decision can be complicated. Your plans can stir up some feelings both for you and for those receiving the news, but there are different ways to go about leaving. You can choose to walk away with your head held high as opposed to in a fiery rage or with your shoulders slumped. Consider taking a few important steps during your departure to make the transitional journey as smooth as it can be.

Write a Resignation Letter. Regardless of where you work, it is good practice to document your departure while also giving a clear time frame for how much longer you'll be around. (Typically people give themselves about two weeks to wrap up and transition out.) However, this does not take the place of a face-to-face conversation with your boss. These convos can feel awkward, so bring the focus back to gratitude. Even in the worst jobs, you can find something to be grateful for. After all, everything is an opportunity to grow.

Inform Your Coworkers. Colleagues and bosses might really want to know why you're leaving and where you're going, but it's up to you to determine how much or how little you share. A simple *"I decided I was ready for a change"* is a completely valid response.

Do the Work until You Leave. Try not to get too much senioritis and honor the work that needs to get done while you are still in your position.

Quitting a job is totally normal. As uncomfortable or awkward or tense as it may feel to do, it happens all the time and is an important part of the adulting process.

A Moment of Reflection

As we got up close and personal with aspects of that daily grind, we learned a few things about what it means to really make the hustle work:

+ Finding a career trajectory isn't about finding your passion but rather about finding your values and how they can help guide you toward work that actually matters to you.

+ Every workplace has woven its own cultural web, and you will start to find your place in it by establishing important relationships, bringing forth your inner boss.

+ "Playing the game" doesn't have to mean selling your soul; be aware that office politics are a thing that you can navigate with sincerity and values.

+ There are plenty of funky dynamics to work with when it comes to bosses and coworkers, but you can step into them with the grace of an Olympic figure skater.

+ When work isn't what you were hoping for, you can choose to stay or choose to go. There are legit and valid reasons on each side of the coin. Let your values be your guide!

"*Money is only a tool. It will take you wherever you wish, but it will not replace you as the driver.*"

—*Ayn Rand*

CHAPTER FIVE

I Just Found Five Dollars in My Pocket!

Yes, this is the chapter about finances, and yes, that might have you saying, *"Thank u, next,"* but no, it doesn't have to be that way. As a therapist, I've learned that folks tend to avoid the things that make them most uncomfortable. For a lot of people, money comes with discomfort. We are often taught that it's impolite or unsavory to talk about money. That's part of why it's so *taboo* to talk about. Another thing I've learned as a therapist: If something is considered a taboo, that means it's worth talking about. And money is no exception. So, strap in, y'all, because we are about to look this sucker right in the eyes.

How to Not Live Paycheck to Paycheck

Though it's one of the most widespread trends in America, most folks would say they don't love living the paycheck-to-paycheck (PTP) life. Living PTP typically comes with boatloads of stress and a narrow view of the future. The big danger of existing in the PTP world is drowning at the first sign of trouble. Nobody can survive in the middle of the ocean without some sort of floatation device.

What to Do with Cash

Moving away from that PTP life all starts with being able to figure out what the heck to do with all that cheddar. The adult-y answer to this question is budgeting. Learning how to budget for real is often easier said than done, so it's important to be realistic. Start by identifying what you *need* money for—in other words, keep track of what bills need to get paid. Paying bills will always, always, *always* be the first answer to the question of what to do with the money you're making: rent, utilities, transportation (this means car payments, insurance payments, bus/train tickets, bridge tolls, etc.), health insurance, internet, groceries, and anything else you need each and every day. Mapping out a true-blue budget that actually makes sense for you is one of the best things you can do to move away from PTP living. It's also the first step to understanding your spending habits and figuring out how to cut back on throwing money toward things that aren't actual needs.

With your budget in mind, you can start to rein in your spending. Even freeing up a few dollars here and there is what gets you on the road to a wider future. With those extra dollars you can start to do things like chip away at debt and bulk up an emergency fund. At first the cutback can be challenging, but once you get into a flow, you'll start to notice ways to save just about everywhere. Cutting back is totally doable without having to live under a rock and deprive yourself of all things fun. One helpful tip is to cut back in increments. Rather than completely cutting out drinks with friends, start by reducing things bit by bit across the board; $10 here and $20 there can build more quickly than you might think.

With that extra money, you're going to start noticing that you are able to set some aside each month. This is how you start building your emergency fund. At first, think about an emergency fund as equivalent to one paycheck; that's how much you want to have in the bank just in case of "oh crap" moments. And let's face it, life comes with plenty of "oh crap" moments. Even if you start by putting aside only $50 per paycheck, your confidence will begin to boost. The key here is not to take dips in that savings pool once it starts growing. Seeing money in the bank can make your eyes grow wide with spending possibilities. Remind yourself that the money in that pool is not for now; it's your flotation device for later. For many folks, this means finding ways to make that money harder to access, such as by opening a savings account at a different bank or even putting the money into a different type of account that you can't touch at all. The big question that comes up for everyone who is working on a financial flotation device is, *"Do I save, or do I pay down my debt?"* The answer is both.

Debt sometimes keeps you from saving by requiring a monthly payment, meaning that money you could be saving is going toward paying off that debt. The way to end this as quickly as possible is to stop using your credit card(s) altogether. Put a good chunk of your paycheck toward getting rid of that debt while saving what you can, even if it means only $10 or $20 a month is getting saved and the rest is going to your credit card payment. Only after you are debt-free can you truly start to bulk up your savings and get to a place of financial security and opt out of the PTP life.

The Art of Credit Cards

Credit cards are tricky little buggers. They come with all types of exciting rewards, points, and benefits that draw you in. However, they also come with risks. Let's start with how they work in the first place. Credit cards offer their users a specific credit limit that they can spend. When you use a credit card, you are borrowing from a bank to make a purchase. Then you get to choose how much you pay back of what you borrowed each month: the minimum required, a partial amount, or the full amount. If you choose to repay any less than the full amount that you borrowed, interest starts to accumulate.

Interest is a certain amount of money you have to pay *in addition to* what you borrowed in the first place based on how much you owe. When it comes to credit cards, the official term used is *annual percentage rate* (APR). For example, if you bought something for $500 on your credit card and only made a credit card payment of $300, you would have an outstanding balance of $200. If your APR was 10 percent, you would have to pay an extra $20 in addition to the $200 that you owe. Why? Because 10 percent (the APR) of $200 (your outstanding credit card balance) is $20. So now you owe a total of $220. This example is on a super small scale. Where people get into big trouble is when they ignore their credit card balances or only make minimum payments so their total balance remains high.

Don't get too freaked out, though, because there are some great upsides to using credit cards in a responsible way. When used responsibly, credit cards are a great way to build credit, earn rewards, and keep track of your cash flow. Here are the best ways to reap the rewards of credit card usage:

Build Credit by Paying off Your Bill Right Away in Its Entirety. This will keep you from having to pay any interest and will show the credit bureaus what a responsible borrower you are, which will boost your credit score. It's sort of like gaining street cred so that other people will know you're trustworthy and want to work with you.

Earn Rewards by Using a Credit Card for Budgeted Purchases. However, the only way for this to actually work is to use your credit card on what you can actually afford to pay off in full. Once you start to have to pay interest, it totally cancels out any potential rewards you'd be earning.

Pay for Everything with a Credit Card and Pay It off in Full Each Month. By doing this, you can easily see how much you're spending each month and what you're spending it on. This sort of tracking can help a lot of people manage their budget.

Notice a theme? If you guessed, *"I have to be able to pay off my credit card bill, in full, every, single, month,"* ding ding ding! We have a winner! When it comes down to it, the art of credit cards is about the art of discipline. If not used responsibly, credit cards can easily land you in a whole lot of financial trouble.

What to Do When Your
Credit Card Is Maxed Out

Maxing out a credit card isn't the end of the world, but it is a pretty serious thing that's not to be ignored. There are all sorts of reasons for maxing out a card, so it's nothing to be ashamed of. Whatever the reason, there is a two-part solution. The first part involves some self-awareness in understanding what brought you to this point and getting the mental or emotional support you might need to help navigate a propensity toward overspending.

The second part is the practical stuff, beginning with stopping use of all credit cards. Then follow up quickly by getting real about your budget and slashing it by being honest about needs versus wants. This will ultimately help you live frugally in order to pay off more than the minimum payment required on your credit card bill. It might sound intense, but that's why you start with really bringing down your monthly expenses. Instead of spending money on going out with friends, you can take that $50 and put it toward paying down that debt. This doesn't mean staying home and living on rice and beans. It simply means being extremely mindful about your spending and getting creative in order to have fun *and* spend less. This is what you need to do to get yourself out of what could turn into a pretty deep financial pit.

Your Trusty Checking and Savings Accounts

Long gone are the days when people were all paid in cash and brought that cash straight home to be placed in their piggy banks. Though some jobs continue to deal in cash, the majority of people are paid by check or direct deposit, and when the paychecks are coming in, they have to go somewhere. Checking accounts are always open for business and are what gets tapped when you deposit or write checks or use your debit card, an ATM, or a payment app like Venmo. Because carrying cash is less common these days, checking accounts act as cash replacements. Be wary, though—some banks require a minimum account balance, and it is possible to overdraw from these accounts, resulting in overdraft fees. Watching your checking account dwindle and then replenishing it with your next paycheck can give you a pretty clear idea of what living paycheck to paycheck looks like. But because you aren't about that PTP life and want to move in the direction of financial security and stability, you are going to welcome in that sweet, sweet savings account.

Savings accounts are exactly what they sound like. They are the accounts that are really meant to help you prep for big purchases or emergencies, which is why they are separate from your checking account. More often than not, when folks first open a bank account, it is a form of savings account. Sometimes a caregiver opens an account to help a child learn to save, or maybe a teenager wants a place to stash some cash. However you come to it, a savings account is one of the best places to store the money you have that doesn't need to go toward paying your bills. When looking at your current or a potential savings account, there are two big things you want to take stock of:

1. The interest rate or annual percentage yield (APY)—this is what ultimately helps your money grow.

2. Fees or minimum balances required—this is what could potentially ding you.

Each banking institution (bank, credit union, or online-only account) does things a little differently, so it's worth paying attention to these two things in order to pick the best savings account for you. It can really behoove you to take the time to do basic research and shop around for the best numbers. Typically, the big national banks aren't the ones with the best saving rates, so check out online-only banks and local/smaller institutions like credit unions or regional banks.

Money Management Technology

One of the awesome things about tech is how much easier it has made it to learn about, understand, and manage your money. Goodness knows that smartphones and all the fabulous apps available on them have made things easier than ever. Want to order Thai food, get bookshelves hung, talk to your family in Argentina, improve your French, or try a new workout? Done, done, done, done, and done. You can do almost anything from your smartphone, and managing your money is no different. What's more is that many of them are offered to you at the amazing deal of FREE.99!

According to reviews from all over the map, one of the best places to get started is with the well-known, widely used, and highly praised app Mint. Mint continues to get tons of recognition for a few reasons. The biggest thing it does is really help you follow your spending to get a full picture so you can budget and plan. By connecting with your various accounts, it brings everything into one place so that you can see everything from money in the bank to bills that need to get paid to credit scores. With all that info in one place, Mint can help you set a budget for yourself and stick to it. In addition, it offers educational resources to help grow your knowledge, and you know what they say … knowledge is power. On the other hand, if using a budgeting app isn't the best fit for you, NerdWallet also offers great suggestions for downloadable spreadsheets to help you manage your money with a hands-on approach.

How to Save and Invest for the Future, Even When It's Hard

You might be sick of hearing it already, but when it comes to preparing for retirement, saving is important. I mean, you want to retire, right? Hey, maybe you're the "I'm gonna last forever" type. If that's you, more power to ya, but eventually we all sort of have to retire from the workforce. Fact of life: We all age out of work eventually. So, before you start snoozing on me, do yourself a favor and take a look at these basic ways to save and invest. Living your best 70-year-old life depends on you!

IRAs

You may have heard something about IRAs but have no idea what they actually are. An IRA is an individual retirement account, and they come in all sorts of flavors. There's a traditional IRA, Roth IRA, nondeductible IRA, SEP, and a SIMPLE IRA. Regardless of your flavor, they are really clutch because each helps you save for the future while getting you some tax benefits in the present. The two big players in the IRA game are the Roth and the traditional, so we'll hang out with those for now.

The traditional IRA is all about that tax-deductible life. It means if you are contributing money to this account, you can deduct these contributions from your overall taxes and save some money in the moment. This allows you to grow your money by not paying the taxes on it now and instead paying them later when you withdraw that cash (aka when you retire). The Roth IRA, on the other hand, is all about that nondeductible life. This means that instead of taking that sweet money-saving tax deduction now (like with the traditional IRA), a Roth IRA lets you save later by not taxing any of the money you withdraw from the account during retirement.

Deciding which IRA is right for you is about looking at the details to compare and contrast things like how soon you need to access the funds (hopefully not soon), how much of what you contribute to the account can you deduct on your taxes in the present, and where you imagine yourself to be financially in retirement. At the end of the day, saving for retirement is saving for retirement. So whichever IRA flavor you go with is still a good choice.

401(k)s

A 401(k) is the type of retirement plan that you are most likely to
see in a benefits package for a job, but how many people actually
know what on Earth it's about? Why do employers make it such a
big deal as a benefit? Two words: *compound interest*. Okay, one more
word: *matching!*

First and foremost, a 401(k) retirement plan is a specific account
that is funded straight from payroll *before* any taxes have been taken
out. Then the money in this account is invested into a number of
different stocks, bonds, mutual funds, and more. The kicker? None
of the money you gain is taxed until you start using it in retirement,
so it can grow and grow and grow. This is that sweet compound
interest that can really boost someone who starts an account like a
401(k) when they're young. It means there's a lot more time for the
money to grow.

That third special word that can often come with a 401(k) is *matching*.
Sometimes employers set you up with your trusty 401(k) account
and then match a percentage of whatever you decide to put into it,
oftentimes somewhere between 2 and 5 percent. For the sake of ease
(this stuff can already make your head spin), let's say your employer
offers a 401(k) match of 5 percent of your annual income and that
income is $60,000. That means your employer is down to contrib-
ute a max of $3,000 every year to your 401(k). The catch is they'll
only contribute that much if they are matching what you're already
putting in. To maximize this benefit, you also have to contribute
your own $3,000 (or 5 percent) of your annual salary. Now, just like
that, you have $6,000 in your 401(k) instead of the $3,000 you put in

on your own. It might not sound like much, but over the years, that 5 percent match can make a big difference. If you think back to that sweet, sweet compound interest, that's free extra cash from your employer that helps you build your nest to chill in when retirement comes around.

What Does a Bad Investment Look Like?

There are also those investments that are better described as "investments" because they lack legitimacy. For example, if your buddy is cajoling you to throw $500 down on a fantasy football league because the final pool is $5,000 and he's got "insider knowledge," you might want to think twice before diving in. What are the odds that you're actually going to see any of that $5K or even get your $500 back? The funkier the bargain, the worse the odds. The same is true for giving people chunky "loans." I know it can be hard to say no to a friend or family member when they come to you, but think about where else could you put that $500. Paying down debt? Saving for the future? Boosting your emergency fund? Keeping an eye out for bad investments is another way to move away from a paycheck-to-paycheck lifestyle and toward greater financial security.

When you're ready to truly invest your money, consider a few things. Questioning the best use for your money, your investing objectives, how much time you have for your money to grow, and your risk tolerance are all ways to decipher between good investments and lousy ones.

Bad investments are the ones that don't match your answers to these questions. For example, if you're 24 and feel comfortable giving your money plenty of time to safely and conservatively grow before you'll need to access it again, it would be ill-advised to invest a good chunk of change in something that is high-risk and has short-term objectives.

Taxes

Unless you work in the world of finance, you probably hardly think about taxes until you find yourself wondering, "Oh shoot! Did I file?" Even if you're on top of those W-2s and TurboTax is bookmarked as one of your favorite tabs, you might not know much about taxes. One of the main questions everyone is curious about when they see their income before and after taxes is, "Where is my tax money going?"

Really, Where Is My Tax Money Going?

But for real, everyone deserves to understand why they work their tush off only to have some of that income collected by federal, state, and sometimes local governments. It can feel super frustrating to see your income dwindle after taxes are taken out. However, with an understanding of why your income gets taxed in the first place, you can breathe a little more easily. Taxes are really about all citizens contributing to the place where they live. You've heard the saying, "It takes a village," right? Well, it literally does. It takes everyone in the country to help the country run. On the national scale, there are four major items that you contribute to as a citizen by way of your tax dollars: social security (to care for those people who are no longer working), defense and security (e.g., the Department of Defense and Homeland Security), major health programs (Medicare, Medicaid, and the Children's Health Insurance Program), and safety net programs such as housing assistance, food stamps, and unemployment.

At the state level, things differ because each state determines how taxes are spent. However, there are a handful of ways that almost every state uses tax dollars. The two biggest items for nearly every state are education and health care. K–12 schools, community colleges, universities, and vocational institutions get a major chunk of funding from their states. Similarly, states also help fund important health insurance programs like Medicaid and the Children's Health Insurance Program. The rest of the tax dollars go toward all kinds of important public systems like transportation, corrections facilities and programs, and low-income assistance.

People have all sorts of different feelings about where their tax money is going. Regardless of your feelings about *how* those tax dollars are spent, what matters is the understanding of *why* paying your taxes is an important civic duty. At the end of the day, taxes are about how you contribute to the awesome place where you live. Whether it is at the local, state, or national level, rather than carrying a sense of dread, think of taxes as one of the ways in which you are an active part of your community. Next time you see children running around on an elementary school playground, drive down a freshly paved road, or have the urge to wave at a fire truck rolling by, you can remind yourself, "Heck yeah! I am part of making these awesome things happen!"

How to Prepare Your Taxes: The Basics

You are living in one of the greatest days and ages for filing taxes because of all the tech offerings that make filing easier than it's ever been. From TurboTax to H&R Block to the IRS itself having its very own online filing platform, you totally have the tools you need to be your very own tax expert. That said, it can be intimidating to file your own taxes, so if it feels more comfortable for you, you can absolutely meet with a tax guru (also known as an accountant) to help you out. The main downside to going this route is that accountants can be fairly pricey. Unless you've got the funds or a hookup, you might want to try your hand at filing solo. Don't trip—you can absolutely do it, and once you do, it can feel pretty damn empowering to know that you handled it on your own.

Here's how to make it happen: Tax Day is April 15, so, in January and February, people start to gather the info they need to file their taxes. The good news is that employers are on their game and know when it's time to provide you with the info you need (typically a W-2 form). If you have any other financial bits to take into account (student loans, financial investments, interest earnings, self-employment), the forms you need to file will still come your way. (If they don't, contact those institutions and ask for them.) Once you've got all the financial info you need to file, take some time with one of the many online tools at your disposal. TurboTax is one of the most widely used and trusted platforms. It is super user-friendly and will walk you through each and every step. What's more, nearly all of the online filing platforms are prepared to answer questions that come up along the way. When it comes to filing taxes, the IRS is 100 percent available to help you. Check it out by going straight to the source: IRS.gov. It can be time-consuming but so very worth it. If doing your own taxes and being financially savvy and empowered AF doesn't do it for you, you can always throw a party to get them done. Decorate your house with plenty of power strips so everyone can plug their laptops in without blowing a fuse! Bake a cake! Filing your own taxes is something worth celebrating.

What to Do If You Owe

There are all kinds of reasons why you might owe the IRS when tax time comes around. To keep it simple, we are going to assume that you have one job with one employer. The more you throw into the mix (multiple sources of income, self-employment, etc.), the more complicated the tax situation gets. On this simpler route, the most common reason someone might owe would be related to your withholdings.

Think back to when you first started your job. Remember that weird little form you filled out with all the boxes? It may have been sort of confusing, and when you turned it into whoever hired you, you may have had a shoulder-shrug moment of *I think I did this right.* That nifty little form is a W-4. This one-pager lets your employer know how much to take out of your paycheck to cover taxes. If you decide that you don't want your employer to take too much out of your paycheck for taxes (which gives you more money in each paycheck), that means your withholdings are smaller. If you withhold too little from your paycheck for taxes, you will end up owing because you weren't paying those taxes throughout the year. However, if you withhold a lot from your paycheck, you end up overpaying taxes. And that, my friend, is how returns happen.

What to Do If You Get a Return

So, you slayed your civic duties by throwing yourself a tax party to file on time and get yourself squared away. When you're ready to submit, you see that the feds *and* state are going to be sending you a nice chunky check or direct deposit right into your bank account. Hell yes! Now *that* is something to celebrate. You can finally take that trip you've been fantasizing about, buy that gaming system you've been itching to get, or…*stop!* Stop right there! Before you start making it rain, let's make a U-turn and head back to the beginning of this chapter where we got up close and personal with that whole not-living-paycheck-to-paycheck thing. Yeah, remember that? Well, receiving a tax return can play a starring role in important financial moves like paying down debt, cushioning your emergency fund, or throwing a good extra chunk into savings for the future.

Another way to respond to getting a tax return is to remember that refunds are not bonuses. It can feel that way when all of a sudden you've got an extra $3,000 in your hands. However, this isn't a little extra icing on top. It's a return of what was yours to begin with. Getting a refund means you overpaid. You wouldn't pay $100 for your morning coffee and wait a year for $95 to get returned to you, right? Think of all the other things you could be doing with that $95 (read: *saving*). If you find yourself getting big fat returns, think about tweaking that nifty little W-4 form. Adjusting your tax withholdings will result in a smaller refund and put your money back in your pocket in order to make it work for you in the moment.

Debt Is a Four-Letter Word

There are some pretty icky words in the English language, but one of the ickiest out there is *debt*. This bummer of an experience not only *can* happen to most of us but likely will. Because there are so many ways to get into a financial hole, it's important to know the differences between good debt and bad debt. Ultimately, the difference is about what the debt is doing to or for you. Good debt is the kind that can actually help you get closer to your life goals by helping increase either your earning potential or your net worth. Examples of good debt are student loans and home mortgages.

On the other hand, there's bad debt—the big, yucky, slimy, fire-breathing dragon type of debt that keeps you locked away in a dungeon and blocks you from accomplishing all your badass financial goals. This can often look like significant credit card debt, personal loans for unnecessary expenses like vacations, expensive habits, and payday loans. What's tricky is that bad debt can come out of some of those good debts. Not all student loans and home mortgages can propel you forward. That's why it's important to keep your eye on interest rates and research multiple options before deciding to take on a debt. However, if it's too late for that and the debt is already there, fear not! There are absolutely things you can do to get yourself out of that money pit.

Step 1: Look Your Debt Straight in the Eye

First and foremost, start by high-fiving yourself for even getting to this point. There are tons of people who would much rather look away when it comes to money matters, but you're here now, and that's what's important.

Start by laying it all out on the table. Literally. Sometimes it helps to simply put pen to paper and make a list. Write down the names of all of the financial institutions that you owe money to and the amounts you owe. Then, make note of each of their interest rates (APRs) and the minimum payments required. Finally, take a deep, deep breath. Actually, take a few. Seeing it all laid out in front of you might be overwhelming at first, but don't worry, you're already on the right path.

Step 2: Use a Spreadsheet or Budgeting App

Don't feel the need to make yourself bonkers by reinventing the wheel and trying to figure out the best way to make a spreadsheet. There are tons of apps and spreadsheets already at your fingertips to help you get the full picture *and* execute your plan of attack all in one place. Again, Mint is a great free budgeting app. It also allows you to make custom payoff goals and then guides you toward those goals since it knows all of your budget info already.

For those who prefer to be a bit more hands-on, there are tons of great spreadsheets that folks have created and shared for free. When you use a template, you don't have to worry about coming up with all the difficult Excel functions on your own. They come ready for you to plop in your own numbers and then do all the math for you. Some of them even come with their own suggestions on how to pay down your debts. One option for paying down your debt is known as the "snowball" method. This method is all about paying down your smallest debts first. Going the "snowball" route is a little easier to implement, and you do tend to see results more quickly. Some of the best spreadsheets for the "snowball" method are the Debt Reduction

Calculator by Vertex42 and the Debt Reduction Spreadsheet by Squawkfox. Once you are geared up with the right tech to support you, you're ready to go to battle.

Step 3: Attack!

Getting out of debt all starts with returning to your budget so you can cut spending to have more money to use to pay down your debts. Once you have a sense of those resources, another great game plan suggests you start with paying off debts with the highest interest rates (APRs). This is known as the "avalanche" method. If you have multiple debts, of course, you will continue to make the minimum payments on each of them. While the "snowball" method is a totally doable place to start, focusing on the credit card with the highest interest should be your priority.

One of the simpler strategies to implement is to cut out credit card spending completely. The best way to stop your debt from growing is to stop using the things that put you there in the first place. At the same time, if those high interest rates are making it damn near impossible to pay down debt, another useful strategy is to look into lowering your interest rates, whether through debt consolidation or simply giving your creditor a call to ask for a lower rate. At the end of the day, the quickest way to make it happen is to earn more and spend less. Pick up a side gig, sell the things you don't need, and change up your day-to-day habits.

A Moment of Reflection

Hot damn did we cover a boatload of major money knowledge! Let's take a minute to look at what we gained from just the tip of the finance iceberg:

+ Living paycheck to paycheck not only sucks but puts you in a pretty vulnerable position, so you want to start stashing money away as soon as you can to give yourself a good cushion.

+ There are two saving vehicles, IRAs and 401(k)s, that are future-focused and meant to help support you in your retirement.

+ Not only are taxes how each of us pitches in to be a good citizen of our state and country, but they are also totally manageable to file with all of the great resources out there.

+ Budgeting might be tough, but bad debt is tougher. That means keeping an eye on your cash flow and being smart about credit cards.

"There is no better experience in the world, than the world itself."

—*Robert D. Goldstein (a.k.a. my dad)*

CHAPTER SIX

How to Adult Like You Mean It

Hey now, look at you! End of the book! After five sweet chapters, your brain is chock-full of delicious adulting nuggets, and you're ready to turn that knowledge into action. This is where the magic really happens. That whole "knowledge is power" thing— it's true. It's time to tap into your most powerful self by bringing all the learning, awareness, and new skills to life.

Putting It All Together

As you start to make the magic happen, let's recap the ingredients you're working with. The first major ingredient was recognizing where you were starting and where you were headed. In plain language, you had to get real with yourself about your current state of adulting and identify the changes you want to make. Once you got a sense of your starting point, we tuned into the You Show. Lots of people have lots of opinions, but in order to start adulting like you mean it, the focus has to do a 180 from them to you: recognizing *your* wants, *your* needs, and *your* dreams, and prioritizing the hell out of them. Others might think they know what you should be doing, but focusing on the "shoulds" never did anybody any good. The focus shifted to getting your basic needs met. That means finding the best ways to nurture and care for your physical self *and* your mental self. Lest you forget how important a well-nurtured mind is!

From there, we opened things back up to make sense of the adulting process in the context of others. The universe doesn't exist in a vacuum, and neither do you, so you had to start thinking about those major relationships: familyships, friendships, and partnerships. Alright, people, get ready for it, we are about to make our first major link: There is no way to separate your relationship with yourself from your relationships with others. They are all connected. Circle of life and all that. But really, Mufasa had a great point when he reminded Simba that everything exists in a delicate balance. This is where you can start to find the right balance for yourself. As you prioritize and care for you, there is a greater likelihood of accessing the ability to navigate relationships with others in ways that feel healthy. Think of it as a cycle. You feel good, your relationships feel good, which keeps you feeling good, and so on and so forth. Pro tip: *Good* doesn't always mean positive. Feeling good means staying grounded and embracing the harder stuff in order to learn, grow, and come out the other side.

After connecting the relationship with yourself to your relationship with others, you took a look at what it means to truly *do work*. Funny little thing about relationships: They don't stop at your personal life. Oh no. They extend far and wide into that place where you spend a big ol' chunk of your time: work. Chapter 4 started with returning the focus to you, because finding solid ground at work means accessing that beauteous relationship with yourself in order to stay connected to the things that matter most to you (*cough cough* values *cough*). Then what happened? Surprise, surprise—the lens widened again to look at others and how they factor in. At work, relationships with others make a massive difference. Finding that balance between you and your managers/bosses/coworkers is how you slay the game. Feel free to look back at that relationship chapter and see if you can apply any of it to work. (I'll tell you a secret…you can.) All relationships—personal, professional, or somewhere in between—have the ability to ebb, flow, transition, build us up, bum us out, and be rooted in love and respect.

Are you noticing a trend in what it might take to adult like you mean it? Re-la-tion-ships! Damn right. Well, and some general knowledge about money and everyday "domestic" stuff. It's hard to engage in healthy relationships with ourselves and others when we're struggling to make ends meet or maintain a comfy, cozy living situation. Turning this knowledge into action is about understanding what it is to *practice*. For many years, people have used this phrase: *"Practice* *makes perfect."* I'm here to tell you to toss that sh*t right out the window. Practice does *not* make perfect because there's no such thing as perfect. What practice really makes is progress. And none of us are ever truly done progressing. If we ever reached perfection, we'd stop. Now, I don't know about you, but I'm pretty sure Serena Williams doesn't simply step onto the court, play her heart out, and win 23 Grand Slams. No. She practices. She progresses. Time and time again. *That* is what turning knowledge into action is all about: returning to an active practice over and over and over again in order to continue to progress. Because until time machines are invented and widely available, all we have is our ability to continue to move forward.

So, you read these pages, you pondered these words, and you started putting them into action. Now it's time to see where you feel like you've grown. I know how easy it is to get sucked into the idea that you have to get all the answers on this quiz "right." But the truth is, there is no right or wrong here and certainly no good or bad. Similar to the quiz you started with, it's about gathering honest information about where you're at to use as a continuous guide to where you want to go.

JUST HOW "ADULT" AM I NOW?

1. I am striking a balance between eating hot chips and my favorite fruit.
- ○ True
- ○ False

2. I know at least three ways to nurture my body.
- ○ True
- ○ False

3. I believe that my thoughts and feels are legit.
- ○ True
- ○ False

4. I can find a balance between prioritizing others and prioritizing myself.

○ True

○ False

5. I have at least two people to turn to when I'm trippin'.

○ True

○ False

6. I have a decent vocabulary to describe what I'm feeling.

○ True

○ False

7. I understand the pros and cons of credit cards.

○ True

○ False

8. I have a savings account where I regularly deposit money.

○ True

○ False

9. I can better set boundaries with my family, even when it's hard.

○ True

○ False

10. I have a sense of who my real friends are.

○ True

○ False

11. I can communicate my thoughts and feelings to a love interest or partner.

○ True

○ False

12. I know what my values are when it comes to work.

○ True

○ False

13. I feel okay having tough convos with my boss.

○ True

○ False

14. I feel like I'm on the path I want to be on, even if it's scary.

○ True

○ False

15. I have a clear sense of what adulting means to me.

○ True

○ False

RESULTS AND EXPLANATION

At this point, if you're blowing through this sucker with "all true" or "all false" results, something's up. Like I said, this is not about getting it right, it's about getting a realistic sense of where you've gone thus far and where else you have to go. If you're looking at a mixture of true and false answers, notice if there's some sort of pattern. Maybe the statements that are true for you happen to be things that are you-focused, and the false responses are more about others. Maybe the reverse is true. Maybe it's the work part of adulting that's proving to be harder than you had originally thought. Maybe you feel solid in the ways in which you go about caring for your physical self.

Whatever patterns you notice, stop and give yourself a second to celebrate. If any of these are starting to feel true, or truer than they were before, you are making moves. It may seem like NBD, but it's not. It's a super BD! What keeps all of us moving forward is recognizing and honoring the steps we take. After all, if you aren't giving yourself cred for the progress you've made, why would you want to make any more? Once you've finished that dance party, eaten that ice cream, or called your grandma for a verbal high-five, you're ready to keep looking forward. If you notice there are still some bits about adulting that are tougher than others, you're doing it right. Humans are meant to always be in motion. When we stop moving, we stop growing. That means there will always, always, *always* be more. But the fact that there is always more does not mean you'll never be good enough at adulting. No, my dear. It means that the potential of you is infinite. Humans are freaking awesome, and you get to tap into that awesomeness anytime you take the next step.

How to Avoid Backtracking

Taking two steps forward and 10 steps backward happens from time to time, and we need to be kind to ourselves during these moments. As my Uncle Fred says, "This *setback* is a *setup* for a comeback!" That said, setbacks don't have to be full-fledged backtracking. In order to keep from undoing all the great progress you've made, you have to notice that things are slipping in the first place. Awareness is key. Are you crankier lately? Getting into more squabbles with fam, friends, partners, or coworkers? Are you feeling like you want to (or are) throwing tantrums? Start by getting curious. The sooner you ask yourself, *"Okay, what is this really about?"* the sooner you'll be back on the adulting path you'd prefer.

When you get curious about what you are thinking, feeling, and doing, you are far more likely to respond in a way that is both intentional and productive. Without this curiosity, people tend to turn into reactors rather than responders. This is also a great time to employ the buddy system. If you notice yourself struggling to adult, don't be afraid to reach out to one of your trusted peeps and inject some intrigue into life and the situation by calling on them to help hold you down. The same way contestants on *Who Wants to be a Millionaire?* get to "phone a friend," you, too, can tap into those intimate relationships when you feel yourself getting stuck or sliding backward.

Just So You Don't Think We're Gonna Leave You Hanging

Rome wasn't built in a day, you can't have one tuchus in two places, and change doesn't happen overnight. Three different ways to say what the sages have been trying to tell us all along: Patience, young grasshopper. This doesn't mean you should never be frustrated. Adulting is a frustrating process, the same way any new skills are when we first start learning them. What's important is that you are well on your way. You are not only moving along in adulting but are adulting thoughtfully and with intention. As I mentioned earlier, it's way more enjoyable to grow when we feel we are making the choice to do so (aka a labor of love) rather than being forced to learn things the hard way. Part of my hope for you is that you feel confident and intrigued enough to take some of those initial steps with guidance from this book. The adulting journey is an ongoing one because, well, you don't ever really stop being an adult once you've become one. Of course, this doesn't mean you stop having fun. I'll let you in on a little secret; I was taught, by some of the smartest folks I know, that the key to being an adult is to never stop playing. Throughout these pages, we've only scratched the surface of some of the major adulting topics. My great hope for you, dearest reader, is that you continue to play and explore through each of them.

That being said, I don't want to leave you hanging, especially when it comes to the tougher stuff. Keeping your bathroom clean is one thing, but figuring out how to break up with an old friend or tell your boss you disagree with them is a different ball game. To help you continue on your way, I've put together a nice chunk of resources for you at the end of the book. If you notice a topic that really spoke to you, hold on to that curiosity and check out other resources that give you a more in-depth look at it. Be it family relationships, career questions, dating, upping your financial literacy, or figuring out the best way to give your wardrobe an adult makeover, the resources span the gamut of books, videos, podcasts, tech tools, and even a community/group to check out. Don't forget that none of us are meant to go at things alone. Sometimes this means exploring these topics with the folks who are already in your life, and sometimes this means exploring with a new community. Either way, adulting becomes a heck of a lot easier when we go at it armed with a solid sense of self, a few solid peeps, and some solid resources.

A Moment of Reflection

Alright, my friends, it's the final recap. This time we aren't reflecting back on a single chapter. No, no. This is the opportunity to speed-read what really went down throughout these pages if you are thinking TL;DR (Too Long; Didn't Read). That's tech speak for *"Here are the highlights."*

+ Other people will always have opinions. Adulting like you mean it means forming your own.

+ Prioritizing yourself doesn't make you selfish; it makes you healthy. Changes in *your* life happen by figuring out what *you* want, not what other people want for you.

+ Your health is not just physical; it's also mental and emotional. Real adulting happens through finding balance in all of these areas.

+ Everything comes backs to relationships because none of us exist in a vacuum.

+ Relationships ebb and flow, transition and evolve, stick around and peter out. All of these are totally okay.

+ Work doesn't have to mean "finding your calling," but it helps when you're doing something that feels important to you.

+ Work comes with tricky challenges. The more comfortable you get with being uncomfortable (to a reasonable extent, of course), the more you'll thrive.

+ Be mindful about money. Only spend the money you actually have, live within your means, and make sure those means include saving.

+ True adulting is about understanding the concepts of *practice* and *progress*. Commit to the process, and growth and evolution will always follow.

+ You are an incredible thing—capable of big thoughts and actions and full of big feelings. Trust them; they will continue to be your guides.

Resources

BOOKS

The Mindful Path to Self-Compassion: Freeing Yourself from Destructive Thoughts and Emotions by Christopher Germer (Guilford Press, 2009)

A great read to guide you down the path to continuing to focus on you.

Things You Should Already Know About Dating, You F*cking Idiot by Ben Schwartz and Laura Moses (Hachette Book Group, 2017)

Though I'm not a fan of the title (it's rude!), this book has solid knowledge nuggets on not only dating but also moving through the process of romantic relationships.

Practice You by Elena Brower (Sounds True, 2017)

This is a great journal and tool to prompt self-reflection and begin to tap into your inner knowing.

A Job to Love by The School of Life (The School of Life Press, 2017)

The School of Life bring us a solid little read that takes a closer look at what it means to find and keep a job you earnestly enjoy.

Why Didn't They Teach Me This in School? by Cary Siegel (CreateSpace Independent Publishing Platform, 2013)

This gem helps you get answers to nearly all the money questions you can muster by breaking things down by spending, investing, debt, and even housing and insurance.

WEBSITES

NerdWallet (money): NerdWallet.com

The Balance (money): TheBalance.com

These are great websites for all things finance related, with tons of great advice from experts who know what's up.

Mindful: Mindful.org

A solid site to learn more about all the places and spaces where you can apply mindfulness.

thredUP (clothing): thredUP.com

Poshmark (clothing): Poshmark.com

Both of these sites are great options for upping your wardrobe game on a budget (and in a way that is sustainable).

FINANCIAL TOOLS

TurboTax (taxes): TurboTax.intuit.com

IRS (taxes): IRS.gov

Both of these sites are go-to resources when you're ready to take on filing your taxes.

Debt Reduction Calculator by Vertex42 (debt): Vertex42.com /Calculators/debt-reduction-calculator.html

Debt Reduction Spreadsheet by Squawkfox (debt): SquawkFox.com /debt-reduction-spreadsheet

Both of these sites are streamlined ways to help you manage and get out of debt using the "snowball" method.

Avalanche Method Calculator by NerdWallet (debt): NerdWallet .com/article/finance/what-is-a-debt-avalanche

NerdWallet offers various budgeting calculators. This one in particular can help you focus in on the avalanche method for paying down your debt.

PODCASTS

Adulting with Michelle Buteau and Jordan Carlos

Michelle and Jordan beautifully real-talk all the things that come with adulting in a way that makes you laugh.

Death, Sex, & Money with Anna Sale

The things society teaches you not to talk about get talked about here with thoughtful inquiry and awesome insight.

Adulthood Made Easy by Real Simple

Real-life answers to real-life questions delivered in a way anyone can relate to.

VIDEOS (TED TALKS)

Rita Pierson: Every Kid Needs a Champion

This video gives a powerful account of the importance of a growth mindset.
TED.com/talks/rita_pierson_every_kid_needs_a_champion/

Brené Brown: The Power of Vulnerability

This video helps explain the power and impact that can come from stepping into your truth.
TED.com/talks/brene_brown_the_power_of_vulnerability

APPS

Calm (mindfulness)

Fit Bod (exercise)

Grid Diary (journaling)

Headspace (mindfulness)

Insight Timer (mindfulness)

Jour (journaling)

Mint (money)

Tasty (cooking)

COMMUNITY

Coa: JoinCoa.com

A mental fitness studio whose mission is to destigmatize mental health by making it as common and proactive as physical health. Coa offerings include classes, therapy, and community.

Values

Acceptance	Courage	Fun
Adventure	Creativity	Generosity
Assertiveness	Curiosity	Gratitude
Authenticity	Encouragement	Honesty
Beauty	Equality	Humility
Caring	Excitement	Humor
Challenge	Fairness	Independence
Compassion	Fitness	Industry
Conformity	Flexibility	Intimacy
Connection	Forgiveness	Justice
Contribution	Freedom	Kindness
Cooperation	Friendliness	Love

Mindfulness	Respect	Sensuality
Open-mindedness	Responsibility	Sexuality
Order	Romance	Skillfulness
Patience	Safety	Spirituality
Persistence	Self-awareness	Supportiveness
Pleasure	Self-care	Trust
Power	Self-control	
Reciprocity	Self-development	

References

"Barack Obama's Feb. 5 Speech." *The New York Times*. February 5, 2008. nytimes
.com/2008/02/05/us/politics/05text-obama.html.

Dweck, Carol S. *Mindset: The New Psychology of Success*. New York: Ballantine
Books, 2009.

First Round Review. "Hit the Emotional Gym—The Founder's Framework for
Emotional Fitness." Accessed May 26, 2020. firstround.com/review/hit-the
-emotional-gym-the-founders-framework-for-emotional-fitness.

Genius. "Everybody Needs Somebody to Love." Accessed July 13, 2020. genius
.com/The-blues-brothers-everybody-needs-somebody-to-love-lyrics.

The Gottman Institute. "John & Julie Gottman—About." Accessed April 29,
2020. gottman.com/about/john-julie-gottman.

Johnson, S. B., R. W. Blum, and J. N. Giedd. "Adolescent Maturity and the Brain:
The Promise and Pitfalls of Neuroscience Research in Adolescent Health
Policy. *The Journal of Adolescent Health 45*, no. 3 (2009): 216–21. doi.org/10.1016
/j.jadohealth.2009.05.016.

Montesorri, M. "The Erdkinder and the Functions of the University by Maria
Montessori." The Montessori Foundation. Accessed July 13, 2020. montessori
.org/the-erdkinder-and-the-functions-of-the-university-by-maria-montessori.

Neff, K. D., and K. A. Dahm. "Self-Compassion: What It Is, What It Does, and
How It Relates to Mindfulness." In *Mindfulness and Self-Regulation*, edited by M.
Robinson, B. Meier, and B. Ostafin, 121–40. New York: Springer, 2014.

NerdWallet. "Make All the Right Money Moves." Accessed July 9, 2020.
nerdwallet.com/?trk=nw_gn_4.0.

Rand, Ayn. *Atlas Shrugged*. New York: Random House, 1957.

Washington Post Staff. "Transcript: Read Michelle Obama's Full Speech from the 2016 DNC." *The Washington Post*. July 26, 2016. washingtonpost.com/news /post-politics/wp/2016/07/26/transcript-read-michelle-obamas-full-speech -from-the-2016-dnc.

Yerkes, R.M., and J. D. Dodson. "The Relation of Strength of Stimulus to Rapidity of Habit-Formation." *Journal of Comparative Neurology and Psychology 18*, no. 5 (1908): 459–82. doi.org/10.1002/cne.920180503.

Index

A

Action planning, 43
Adulting quiz, 7–13, 127–131
Apps
  budgeting, 108–109, 119
  journaling, 30
  meditation, 29

B

Balance, 36–37
Bosses, 91–92
Boundaries, 15, 51
Budgeting. *See* Finances
Burke, Solomon, 46

C

Caravalho, George A., 76
Caregivers, 49–53
Change, 16–19, 38–43
Cleaning, 70
Clothing, 71
Clutter, 25–26
Communication skills, 61–62, 72
Community involvement, 75
Conflict resolution, 64–65
Connection, 28
Cooking, 33–34
Coworkers, 92–94, 97
Credit cards. *See* Finances

D

Dating, 63–64, 73, 74
Debt. *See* Finances
Domestic basics, 70–71
Dweck, Carol, 6

E

Empathy, 62
Exercise, 34–35

F

Family
  parents and guardians, 49–53
  relationship dynamics, 48–49, 68
  siblings, 53–54
Fears, 5–6
Finances
  budgeting, 102–104
  checking accounts, 107
  credit cards, 104–106
  debt, 118–120
  investments, 109–113
  money management, 108–109
  savings accounts, 103, 107–108
  taxes, 113–117
Fixed mindset, 6
401(k)s, 111–112
Free stuff, 74
Friendships, 55–60, 68

G

Gandhi, Mahatma, 27
Goldstein, Robert D., 122
Gottman, John and Julie, 61–62
Growth mindset, 6, 94

H

Help, asking for, 28
Household basics, 70
Hygiene, 71

I

Imposter syndrome, 90
Individual retirement accounts (IRAs), 110
Initiating change in the workplace, 85–86
Introspection, 30–33
Investments. *See* Finances

J

Journaling, 30–31

L

Love, 65–67

M

Meditation, 28–30
Mental health, 27–33, 44
Mentors, 84–85
Mind-body connection, 34–35
Mindfulness, 29
Moderation, 36–37
Money. *See* Finances
Montessori, Maria, xii

N

Needs, 26
Neff, Kristen, 40
Networking, 84
News and media consumption, 75

O

Obama, Barack, 22
Obama, Michelle, 89
Opinions of others, 2–4, 14–15

P

Parents, 49–53
Passions, 78–80, 98
Pets, 71
Physical health, 33–37, 44, 71
Practice, 125–126, 136
Professionalism, 86
Progress tracking, 43

R

Rand, Ayn, 100
Relationships
    family, 48–54, 68
    friends, 55–60
    importance of, 135
    romantic, 60–68
    work, 125
    with yourself, 124–125
Rent, 70
Respect, 65–67
Rest, 28
Retirement plans, 109–112
Romantic relationships, 60–68
Roommates, 70

S

Scams, 74
Self-focus, 24–26, 44, 124, 135
Selfishness, 24
Setbacks, 132
Siblings, 53–54
Social media, 73
Stress-response cycle, 35

T

Taxes. *See* Finances
Therapy, 31–33
Tough love, 39–40
Transportation, 71

V

Values, 26, 66, 80–83
Voting, 75

W

Work
  attire, 71
  bosses, 91–92
  challenges, 135
  communication skills, 72
  coworkers, 92–94
  culture, 83–86, 98
  passions and, 78–80, 98
  politics, 87–90, 98
  projects, 94–95
  quitting, 95–96
  reasons for staying, 95–96
  values and, 81–83

Y

Yerkes-Dodson law, 40

Acknowledgments

I'd like to acknowledge the many folks at Callisto Media and beyond who worked hard to make this book come to life. A particular thank-you to Joe Cho for being a fantastic cheerleader. I also want to acknowledge with the utmost gratitude the beautiful humans who grant me the incredible privilege of bearing witness to their stories and processes of adulting; each of you is a true light. It is a deep honor to walk your paths with you.

About the Author

Jamie Goldstein, PsyD, is a licensed clinical psychologist in the San Francisco Bay area. She received her Master of Arts and Doctor of Psychology degrees in clinical psychology from the Wright Institute in Berkeley, California. Throughout her career, Dr. Goldstein has provided therapy to adolescents and young adults in a variety of settings, including schools, community mental health, private practice, and mental health start-ups. Currently, she maintains a psychotherapy practice in San Francisco, is the acting chairperson for the Continuing Education Committee of the Alameda County Psychological Association, and is the Therapy Experience Lead for the mental health and emotional fitness studio Coa. Across her roles, Dr. Goldstein seeks to honor the voice and truest self of every individual with whom she works.